Neil Dixon and Dorothy Warre

ESSENTIALS
OCR GCSE
Chemistry A

Contents

1. Fossil fuels, such as natural gas (methane), petrol and diesel, consist of compounds called hydrocarbons.

    (a) Explain what is meant by the term **hydrocarbon**. [1]

    _____

    (b) Burning a fossil fuel is an example of a chemical reaction. Which **two** words describe the reaction that takes place when a fossil fuel burns? Put ticks (✓) in the boxes next to the **two** correct answers. [2]

    Respiration ☐

    Combustion ☐

    Reduction ☐

    Oxidation ☐

    (c) Complete the diagram to show what happens when methane burns in pure oxygen. [3]

    (d) Explain what is meant by the term **incomplete combustion**. [1]

    _____

    _____

    (e) Explain why the car industry is spending millions of pounds developing new technologies that will eventually replace the combustion engine. [4]

    _____

    _____

    _____

    _____

    _____

    _____

    _____

    _____

2. This question is about the Earth's atmosphere.

The Earth's first atmosphere was formed by volcanic activity. It consisted mainly of water vapour and carbon dioxide but no oxygen.

(a) Use words from the list to complete the sentences or answer the questions about how the early atmosphere changed. A word may be used once, more than once or not at all.

photosynthesis   **dissolving**   **condensed**   **evaporated**

heated   **cooled**   **respiration**   **combustion**

   (i) As the Earth _____, water vapour _____ and the oceans formed.   [1]

   (ii) Which **two** processes were involved in the reduction of carbon dioxide levels?   [2]

   _____

   (iii) Which process explains why levels of oxygen started to increase?   [1]

   _____

(b) Approximately how much oxygen and nitrogen is in the atmosphere today?   [1]

   Oxygen: _____   Nitrogen: _____

(c) Describe and explain how both human activity and natural causes are changing the composition of today's atmosphere.

   🖉 *The quality of written communication will be assessed in your answer to this question.*   [6]

   _____

   _____

   _____

   _____

   _____

   _____

   _____

   _____

   _____

   _____

3. Scientists have found a correlation between the amount of pollen in the air and the incidence of hay fever in people who have a pollen allergy. Initially, scientists looked at thousands of medical records. The graph below shows what they found. Despite these results, this correlation was considered not to be conclusive and further skin tests had to be carried out.

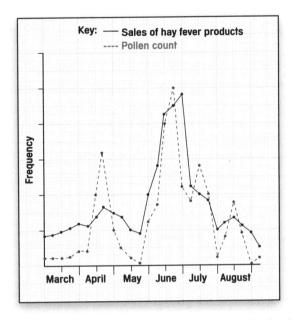

(a) Using the data in the graph, explain what the scientists found and why their results were not considered to be conclusive. [3]

....

....

....

....

....

....

(b) The results from the skin tests are given in the table below.

Skin Test	Hay Fever Sufferers	Non Hay Fever Sufferers
Pollen stuck to skin	Skin became red and inflamed	No visible effect

Explain how these results provide a link between pollen and hay fever. [2]

....

....

....

(c) How would scientists ensure that the evidence collected was reliable, accurate and reproducible? [2]

....

....

....

(d) Asthma is another example of a condition linked to air quality. Studies have shown that when the concentration of nitrogen oxides in the air increases, more asthma attacks occur. However, people still suffer from asthma when levels of nitrogen oxides are very low.

(i) What does this suggest? [1]

....

....

(ii) Suggest **two** factors that scientists need to understand about asthma. [2]

1. ....

2. ....

4. Air pollution is everywhere and it affects us all. We all have a responsibility to reduce it. The two main sources of air pollution are motor vehicles and power stations that burn fossil fuels.

(a) What increases car emissions? Put ticks (✓) in the boxes next to the **two** correct answers. [2]

A fuel-efficient engine	☐	Using low-sulfur fuel	☐
Always driving to the shops	☐	Switching to bio-diesel fuel	☐
Driving a hybrid car	☐	Buying a car with a bigger engine	☐
Using public transport	☐		

(b) By fitting a car with a catalytic converter, the amount of carbon monoxide and nitrogen monoxide entering the atmosphere is reduced. Use the word equations to write balanced symbol equations.

(i) Carbon monoxide + Oxygen ⟶ Carbon dioxide [2]

.... + ... ⟶ ....

(ii) Nitrogen monoxide + Carbon monoxide ⟶ Nitrogen + Carbon dioxide [2]

.... + ... ⟶ .... + ...

(c) What can be used to decrease the emissions from a coal-fired power station? Put ticks (✓) in the boxes next to the **two** correct answers. [2]

Fitting a filter system ◯

Using hydroelectricity to power it ◯

Increasing production ◯

Using oil to power it ◯

(d) Following an international meeting about climate change in Kyoto, Japan, in 1997, people from many countries agreed to reduce carbon dioxide emissions. Targets were set for the individual countries, which continue to meet regularly. The governments of the countries are required to take appropriate measures to meet the targets.

(i) Describe what is being done in the UK on a national and local level to meet these targets and explain how new legislation could have an impact on the local economy.

🖉 *The quality of written communication will be assessed in your answer to this question.* [6]

....

....

....

....

....

....

....

....

....

....

(ii) Suggest why governments in different countries may consider taking different actions to try to reduce carbon dioxide emissions. [2]

....

....

....

....

....

(e) Suggest how an individual person could help to reduce air pollution. [2]

....

....

....

....

5. (a) Many of the pollutants found in the atmosphere are a result of human activity. In parts (i) to (iv) below are the names of four pollutants. Use as many of the following key words as possible to describe where they come from.

power stations   fossil fuels   combustion engine

burning   incomplete combustion   coal

(i) Carbon dioxide: .... [1]

....

(ii) Nitrogen monoxide: .... [1]

....

(iii) Sulfur dioxide: .... [1]

....

(iv) Carbon particulates: .... [1]

....

(b) Complete the table with the formulae of the molecules shown. Use the key to help you. [4]

Name	Formula	Molecule
Carbon dioxide		⊘●⊘
Nitrogen monoxide		●⊘
Water		○⊘○
Sulfur dioxide		⊘⊗⊘

Key: ● Carbon   ⊘ Oxygen   ○ Hydrogen   ● Nitrogen   ⊗ Sulfur

(c) Atmospheric pollutants cannot just disappear; they have to go somewhere. Draw straight lines to show what happens to each of the pollutants. [4]

Pollutant

| Carbon dioxide |

| Sulfur dioxide |

| Carbon particulates |

| Nitrogen oxides |

What happens to it

| Used by plants during photosynthesis |

| Deposited on buildings |

| Reacts with water to form acid rain |

(d) Here is some data about carbon monoxide collected from a city centre:

| Carbon monoxide (ppm) | 5.3 | 5.6 | 5.2 | 5.9 | 5.5 |

(i) Why is the level of carbon monoxide carefully monitored in many city centres? [1]

....

....

(ii) It is not possible to give a true value for the concentration of carbon monoxide but it is likely to lie within the range of the collected data. Complete the statement below about the range of the data. [1]

The range is .... ppm to .... ppm.

[Total: .... / 64]

Higher Tier

6. This question is about gases that are found in the atmosphere.

(a) The early atmosphere was formed by volcanic activity. Over millions of years the atmosphere slowly changed. Today's atmosphere is very different. Describe these differences. [2]

....

....

....

....

(b) The atmosphere began to change when green plants started to grow on Earth. In your own words, explain what you think happened. You will need to include information about how the amount of carbon dioxide and oxygen changed and what caused the changes. [3]

(c) Suggest reasons why today's atmosphere is constantly monitored by scientists. [4]

7. Data are important to scientists because they can be used to test a theory or explanation. Rebecca and Tom collect data to test whether sulfur particulates are an example of a pollutant caused by human activity. They collect the data in the centre of a town and in a country park, on the same day. Their results are shown below.

Time	Concentration of Sulfur Particulates (ppm)	
	Town Centre	Country Park
3.00pm	2.5	0.2
4.00pm	0.3	0.1
5.00pm	3.0	0.1
6.00pm	3.5	0.2

(a) Suggest **three** reasons why it is not possible to find the true value for the concentration of the sulfur particulates. [3]

....

....

....

....

(b) What is the range of values shown in the town centre? [1]

.... ppm to .... ppm

(c) Why is it so important to repeat measurements? [3]

....

....

....

....

....

(d) Which measurement is the outlier in the data? [1]

.... ppm

(e) Work out the best estimate of the true values for each set of results. Show all your working. [4]

....

....

....

....

....

....

....

(f) How do these results relate to the theory that sulfur particulates are an example of a pollutant caused by human activity? [2]

(g) Is there a significant difference between the mean concentrations of sulfur particulates in the town centre and the country park? Give reasons for your answer. [2]

8. The Intergovernmental Panel on Climate Change (IPCC) is concerned about emissions of nitrogen oxides from aircraft.

(a) (i) Why are nitrogen oxides produced in the aircraft engines? [2]

(ii) The reaction takes place in two stages. Complete the equation for stage one. [3]

Nitrogen + Oxygen ⟶ ....

⚫⚫ + ⊘⊘ ⟶ ▭

(iii) During the second phase of the reaction, which process produces the nitrogen dioxide? Put a tick (✓) in the box next to the correct answer. [1]

Combustion ☐   Displacement ☐

Reduction ☐   Respiration ☐

Oxidation ☐

(b) Explain what is meant by the term **NO$_x$**. [2]

(c) Suggest why the IPCC is concerned about NO$_x$ emissions from aircraft. [2]

....

....

....

(d) Since the introduction of catalytic converters on new cars, the levels of NO$_x$ produced in city centres has dropped. Complete the equation to show what happens in a catalytic converter.

Nitrogen monoxide + Carbon monoxide ⟶ .... + ... [3]

9. Sulfur dioxide is produced as a by-product by many coal-fired power stations. It is often removed from the flue gases by wet scrubbing using an alkaline slurry.

(a) How does sulfur dioxide get into power station flue gases? [2]

....

....

....

(b) Complete the following sentence. Use a word from this list. [1]

oxidised   **absorbed**   **reduced**

During wet scrubbing, sulfur dioxide is .... by the alkaline slurry.

(c) Why is it necessary to remove the sulfur dioxide? [2]

....

....

[Total: .... / 43]

1. In everyday life we use many different materials. Some are produced from natural resources; others are produced by chemical synthesis.

   (a) The table below shows different types of material.

   Put a tick (✓) in the correct column to show how each material is produced. [4]

Material	Natural Resources	Chemical Synthesis
Nylon		
Wood		
PVC		
Wool		

   (b) The table below shows some of the properties of the materials. Complete the third column by stating a suitable use for each material. [4]

Material	Properties	Uses
Nylon	Lightweight Stretchy Strong Waterproof	
Wood	Quite a good insulator of heat Hard and rigid Waterproof	
PVC	High tensile strength Tough and durable Not very stretchy Waterproof	
Wool	Medium strength Good insulator of heat Stretchy Adsorbs water	

(c) Strength and elasticity are important properties of a climbing rope. Manufacturers test the fibres before they make them into ropes.

Here are the results of a series of tests of the strength of a nylon fibre:

Test Number	1	2	3	4	5
Strength (kN)	616.0	617.5	616.2	615.9	616.8

(i) Suggest reasons why the test was carried out five times. [3]

....

....

....

....

(ii) What is the range of the data shown in the table? [1]

.... kN to .... kN

2. Crude oil is a very useful raw material. It is a thick, black, sticky liquid made up of a mixture of hydrocarbons.

(a) What is the name given to the process of separating crude oil? Put a tick (✓) in the box next to the correct answer. [1]

Fractional crystallisation ⃞   Fractional decanting ⃞

Fractional distillation ⃞   Fractional partition ⃞

(b) Name the elements present in a hydrocarbon. [1]

....

(c) Different hydrocarbons have different boiling points because their molecular chains are different lengths. Explain why the separation of crude oil depends on this fact. [3]

....

....

....

....

....

....

3. Many leading sports-clothing manufacturers now use antibacterial fibres containing silver nanoparticles in their garments to help keep them fresh. Some experts are worried about the possible effects on the skin of long-term exposure to nanoparticles.

(a) A group of students is talking about nanoparticles.

Darby
A nanoparticle is the width of a human hair.

Gwyneth
A nanoparticle is the width of a few atoms.

Jonathan
Nanoparticles have a large surface area compared to their volume.

Matthew
Nanoparticles have a small surface area compared to their volume.

Deborah
Nanoparticles are polymers.

Which **two** students are making correct statements? [2]

.... and ....

(b) Name **two** other products that use nanoparticles and explain how the nanoparticles change the properties of the material used to make the products.

🖉 *The quality of written communication will be assessed in your answer to this question.* [6]

....

....

....

....

....

....

(c) Suggest why some experts are worried about the possible effects on the skin of long-term exposure to nanoparticles. [3]

....

....

....

....

....

4. A Year 6 class has been asked to design some seats for their playground, so that groups of children can sit down and chat during breaks. The chairs must have these qualities:

- Strong enough to sit on
- Cheap to buy
- Easy to move
- Not dangerous

They have to decide what material to use, so they carry out some tests. Here are the results:

Material	Strength	Density	Cost
Iron	Very strong	High	Medium
Wood	Strong	Medium	High
Polypropene	Strong	Low	Low

After much discussion the majority of the class agreed to choose polypropene.

(a) Suggest why the majority of the class chose polypropene. Use the information in the table to support your answer.

✐ *The quality of written communication will be assessed in your answer to this question.* [6]

....

....

....

....

....

....

....

(b) Some of the class were not happy with the decision because they thought that polypropene was bad for the environment. Which statements explain why? Put ticks (✓) in the boxes next to the **two** correct answers. [2]

Polypropene is made from a non-renewable material. ☐

Polypropene is grown in hot countries. ☐

Polypropene comes in bright colours. ☐

Polypropene can be recycled. ☐

Polypropene is non-biodegradable. ☐

(c) Two members of the class thought that iron chairs would be better in windy weather. Explain why. [2]

[Total: .... / 38]

Higher Tier

5. PVC is produced from small molecules by the process of polymerisation. The diagram represents one of these molecules.

● Carbon   ◉ Chlorine   ○ Hydrogen

(a) What is the chemical formula of the small molecule used to produce PVC? Use the key to help you. [1]

(b) What is the name given to small molecules that can join together to form polymers? Put a tick (✓) in the box next to the correct answer. [1]

Polymers ☐   Repeat units ☐

Minimisers ☐   Monomers ☐

(c) Briefly describe what happens during polymerisation. [2]

(d) Put a tick (✓) in the box next to the diagram that correctly represents part of a PVC molecule. [1]

A ⬤ □

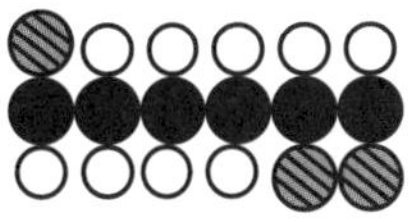

C ⬤ □

B ⬤ □

D ⬤ □

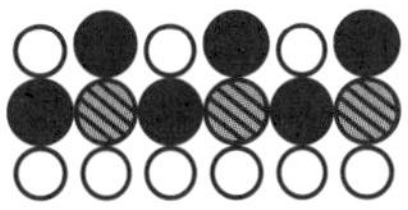

(e) Sometimes manufacturers want to make PVC more flexible, for example so that it can be used to make clothes. They do this by adding a small molecule called a plasticizer. Explain how a plasticizer works. [3]

....

....

....

....

....

6. In industry, the properties of a material are often modified to meet the needs of the application. Naturally occurring rubber used for erasers and rubber bands is soft and weak; vulcanised rubber used for car tyres and shock absorbers is hard and strong.

(a) Which diagram best represents the molecules found in naturally occurring rubber? Put a tick (✓) in the box next to the correct answer. [1]

A □

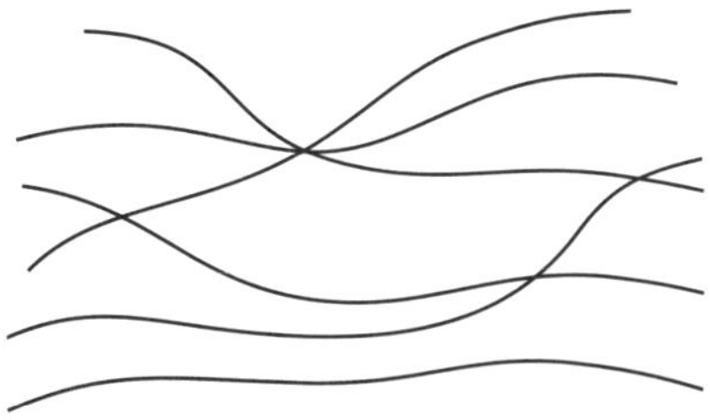

B □

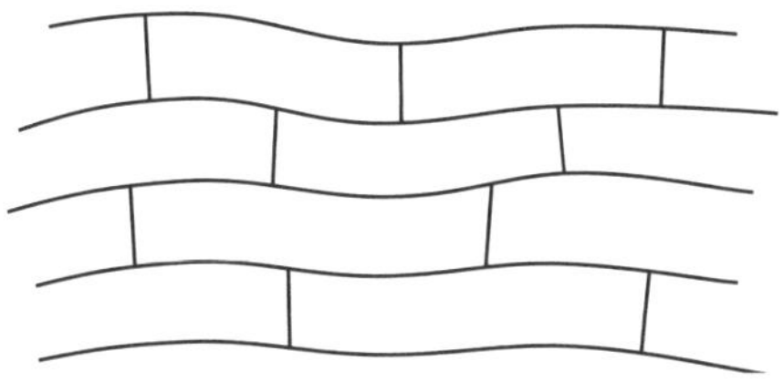

(b) During vulcanisation, sulfur is added to the rubber. What process takes place as a result of this? Put a tick (✓) in the box next to the correct answer. [1]

Polymerisation □

Cross-linking □

Distillation □

Cracking □

(c) Explain why we use vulcanised rubber to make car tyres. You may wish to refer to the diagrams given in part **(a)**. [4]

....

....

....

....

....

7. Nanotechnology is the science of building things on a very tiny scale. Nanoscale materials are designed to do a specific job.

(a) (i) Different objects are different sizes. Put a ring around the object which is the size of a nanometre. [1]

A Earth

B Buckminster fullerene

C Bacterium

D Football field

(ii) Suggest reasons why nanoscale particles are so useful. [3]

....

....

....

....

(b) It is well known that silver has been used for jewellery, coins and decoration for centuries. However, not so many people know that silver was used by the ancient Greeks to purify water and that doctors used to apply a thin layer to wounds to prevent infection and help healing. When antibiotics were invented, doctors stopped using silver to treat wounds. Today, however, dressings containing nanoscale silver particles are being used on patients.

(i) What properties of silver make it good for jewellery? [2]

(ii) Suggest why doctors stopped using silver when antibiotics were invented. [2]

(iii) Suggest why doctors prefer using dressings containing nanoscale silver particles to applying silver directly to the wound.

The quality of written communication will be assessed in your answer to this question. [6]

(iv) Some people are worried about the long-term effects of nanotechnology on human health. Suggest what actions could be taken to address these concerns. [3]

[Total: ____ / 31]

1. People used to believe that features on the Earth's surface were caused by shrinkage when the Earth cooled following its formation. As scientists found out more about the Earth, this theory has been rejected and replaced by tectonic theory.

   (a) Explain what is meant by **tectonic theory**. [2]

   ....

   ....

   ....

   (b) What evidence have scientists found to support tectonic theory? [2]

   ....

   ....

   ....

   (c) (i) Mark clearly on the diagram below where you think that mountains could be formed. [1]

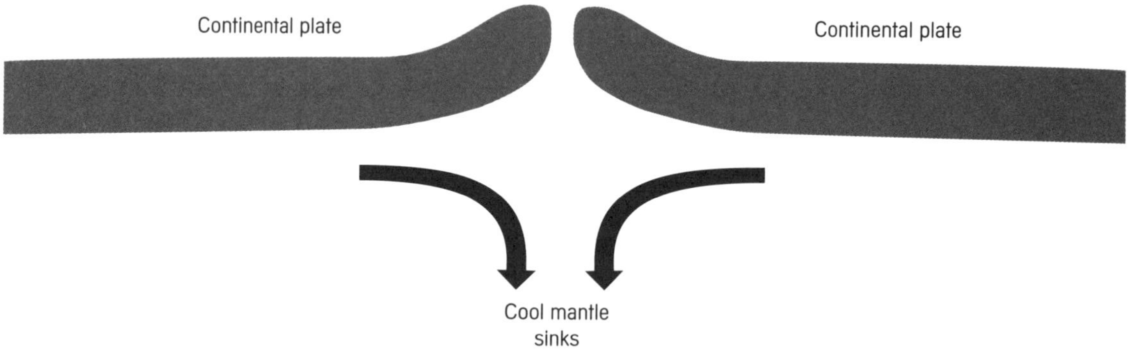

   Continental plate   Continental plate

   Cool mantle
   sinks

   (ii) Explain your answer to part **(i)**. [2]

   ....

   ....

   ....

   ....

(d) The rock cycle plays an important role in the formation of mineral wealth in Britain. There are large deposits of sandstone, a sedimentary rock, found throughout the country.

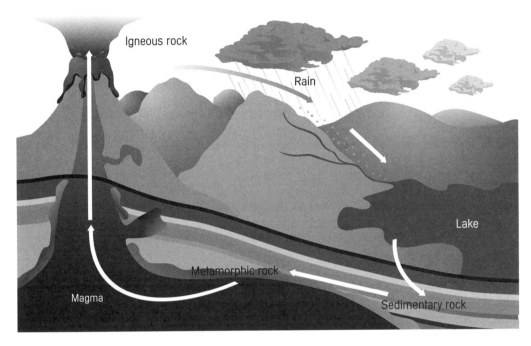

Study the diagram of the rock cycle and then explain how sandstone was formed.

🖉 *The quality of written communication will be assessed in your answer to this question.*   [6]

....

....

....

....

....

....

....

....

2. Salt deposits are found in several areas of Britain. Two different processes are used to extract salt from underground deposits. One method involves mining solid rock salt and is used when the salt is going to be used to treat roads in winter. The other involves solution mining and is used when other chemicals are going to be extracted from the salt.

(a) Here are some statements about the process of mining solid rock salt. They are not in the correct order. Put the statements in the correct order by writing the letters in the empty boxes. [4]

A The rock salt is loaded into a crusher, where it is ground up into small pieces.

B Explosives are used to blast the layer of exposed rock.

C The salt is put into large storage areas.

D A conveyor belt transports the salt to the lift shaft.

E The rock salt is transferred to hoppers and taken to the surface.

Start

(b) What effects does this type of mining have on the environment? [3]

(c) In one major industrial process, an electric current is passed through an aqueous solution of sodium chloride to produce three important chemicals.

(i) What is the name of this process? Put a ring around the correct answer. [1]

Hydrogenation   **Electrolysis**   **Distillation**   **Oxidation**

(ii) Which three chemicals are made during this process? Put ticks (✓) in the boxes next to the **three** correct answers. [1]

Hydrogen ◯   Water ◯

Hydrochloric acid ◯   Chlorine ◯

Sodium chlorate ◯   Sodium hydroxide ◯

(iii) Salt is used in many industries to manufacture a range of different products such as disinfectants, soaps, ceramics, plastics, PVC and margarine. What are the environmental concerns associated with the chemicals you selected in part (ii) that are produced from salt in the manufacture of these products? [3]

3. Salt is an important component of a healthy diet. However, too much salt is not good for you. The Government recommends that an adult should eat 6g of salt a day. Experts estimate that most adults eat between 9g and 10g a day.

(a) The following are statements about salt. Put a tick (✓) in the box next to the statement that is **incorrect**. [1]

Salt is needed to maintain the correct concentration of fluids in the body. ◯

Too much salt can lead to headaches. ◯

Salt in the diet adds taste to food. ◯

Salt plays an important role in the transmission of electrical impulses in the nerves. ◯

(b) Why do food companies add salt to their products? Put ticks (✓) in the boxes next to the **two** correct answers. [1]

To improve the taste ◯

To make the food more healthy ◯

To make the food last longer ◯

To help the cooking process ◯

(c) Eating too much salt increases the risk of heart disease, high blood pressure and strokes. Explain why food companies may not want to lower the amount of salt in their products. [2]

(d) Suggest why it is important to have clear labels on food products. [2]

....

....

(e) How do government departments such as the Department of Health and the Department for Environment, Food and Rural Affairs help to make sure that food is safe, healthy and fairly marketed? [3]

....

....

....

....

4. Every new product has to undergo a life cycle assessment (LCA) that comprises four phases.

(a) What is the purpose of a life cycle assessment? [2]

....

....

(b) What are the four phases in a life cycle assessment? Put a tick (✓) in the box next to the correct answer. [1]

Manufacture, Use, Cost, Disposal ⬜

Development, Making the material from raw materials, Manufacture, Disposal ⬜

Making the material from raw materials, Manufacture, Use, Disposal ⬜

Manufacture, Desirability, Use, Disposal ⬜

(c) All babies need to use nappies and parents have to decide whether to use disposable nappies or reusable nappies. Disposable nappies are made from cellulose fibres, a super-absorbent polymer, whilst reusable ones are made from cloth. To help parents decide, the results of a life cycle assessment are readily available.

Impact (per baby, per year)	Disposable Nappies	Reusable Nappies
Energy needed to produce product	8900MJ	2532MJ
Waste water	28m^3	12.4m^3
Raw materials used	569kg	29kg
Domestic solid waste produced	361kg	4kg

(i) Using the information in the table, which type of nappy is better for the environment? You must give reasons for your answer. [4]

_____

_____

_____

_____

(ii) Which type of nappy do you think most parents choose? Why do you think they make this choice? [1]

_____

_____

_____

[Total: _____ / 42]

Higher Tier

5. The daily recommended amount (RDA) of salt is as follows:

A baby from 0 to 12 months	1g salt per day
A child from 1 to 11 years	2–6g salt per day
An adult	6g salt per day

(a) As a child grows up, what happens to the RDA of salt? Put a tick (✓) in the box next to the correct answer. [1]

Stays the same ☐   Increases ☐   Decreases ☐

(b) The RDA for an adult with high blood pressure is less than 6g salt per day. Which statement best explains why? Put a tick (✓) in the box next to the correct answer. [1]

Salt is needed to help cells take up nutrients. ☐

Too much salt makes you thirsty. ☐

Too much salt can increase the chance of a heart attack. ☐

Salt stops food from going off. ☐

(c) Abigail is 11 years old. This is what she has eaten so far today:

Breakfast   2 crumpets containing a total of 1.1g of salt

               Spread containing 0.2g of salt

Lunch   200g of baked beans containing a total of 1.8g of salt

               2 slices of toast containing a total of 0.7g of salt

               Spread containing 0.2g of salt

(i) Calculate how much salt she has eaten today. [1]

.... g

(ii) If Abigail is going to keep to her RDA of salt, how much salt can she have in her evening meal? [1]

.... g

(iii) Abigail goes out for her evening meal. She can't decide whether to have a beef burger and salad, which contain a total of 1.9g of salt, or chicken tikka masala and rice, which contain a total of 3.5g of salt. Suggest, with a reason, which meal she should choose. [2]

....

....

....

(d) Suggest, with reasons, why some high street restaurants serve meals with more than double the RDA of salt.

The quality of written communication will be assessed in your answer to this question. [6]

....

....

....

....

....

....

6. Alkalis have always been very important chemicals, even before industrialisation.

(a) What were the traditional sources of alkalis? Put ticks (✓) in the boxes next to the **two** correct answers. [2]

Sandstone ◯   Iron ore ◯

Burnt wood ◯   Stale urine ◯

(b) Traditionally, why was it important for the following industries to have a good source of alkali?

(i) The farming industry: _____ [1]

(ii) The textile industry: _____ [1]

(iii) The building industry: _____ [1]

(c) In the 19th century, scientists had to start looking for ways to manufacture alkali to meet growing demand. Early attempts at producing alkali were successful but led to other problems.

The production of alkali from limestone and salt caused the following problems:

- Large volumes of acidic hydrogen chloride gas as a by-product

- Large heaps of waste material

- Foul smelling toxic fumes of hydrogen sulfide from the waste material

Scientists tried to overcome some of these problems by carrying out investigations into the reactions of the by-products.

(i) What was the environmental impact of each of the problems caused by the production of alkali from limestone and salt? [4]

_____

_____

_____

_____

_____

(ii) Suggest why scientists decided to investigate the by-products. [2]

_____

_____

(d) Alkalis react with acids to produce a salt and water. Complete the following word equations.

    (i) Sodium hydroxide + Hydrochloric acid ⟶ .... + Water   [1]

    (ii) Potassium hydroxide + ... ⟶ Potassium sulfate + ...   [1]

    (iii) Sodium carbonate + ... ⟶ Sodium nitrate + Water + ...   [1]

(e) In areas where acid rain is frequent, limestone (calcium carbonate) gravestones suffer more weathering than in other areas. Explain why this happens.   [3]

....

....

....

....

7. The rapid expansion of China's economy, industrialisation and urbanisation, together with a lack of investment in basic water supplies and water treatment, led to widespread water pollution in the 1970s and 1980s. Since then, improvements have been made in many areas but up to a third of the population still do not have access to clean drinking water.

The bar chart below shows the results of a study of water pollution and human health carried out between 1975 and 1986. The people in the control area had access to treated drinking water.

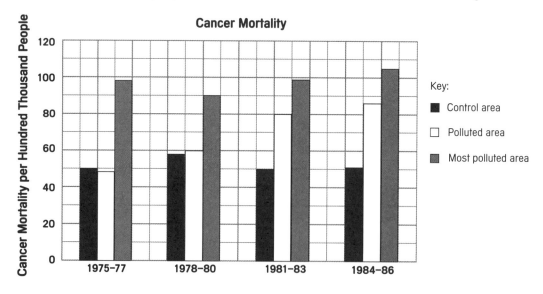

(a) Why did each part of the study include a control area?   [1]

....

....

(b) During the period of the study, how did the number of people dying from cancer change in...

    (i) the control areas? _____ [1]

    (ii) the most polluted areas? _____ [1]

(c) What conclusions can be drawn from the study and what recommendations could be made to the Chinese government? [3]

_____

_____

_____

_____

(d) Twenty years later, the people who carried out the original study revisited some of the previously 'polluted' and 'most polluted' areas. They found that the people living in these areas now had access to drinking water that had been treated with chlorine. Suggest, with reasons, how the number of people dying from cancer and the general health of the population might have changed. Explain your answer.

    🖉 *The quality of written communication will be assessed in your answer to this question.* [6]

_____

_____

_____

_____

_____

_____

_____

_____

8. Many years ago, people used to believe that mountains were formed because the Earth had shrunk in size as it cooled down. Scientists now think that mountains are formed as a result of moving tectonic plates.

(a) Suggest why scientists thought that the Earth had shrunk in size. [1]

_____

(b) What are tectonic plates? [1]

_____

_____

(c) What three pieces of evidence suggest that tectonic plates move? Put ticks (✓) in the boxes next to the **three** correct answers. [3]

The rocks in each continent are very different. ◯

Africa and South America look like two pieces of a jigsaw. ◯

The same fossils are found in different continents. ◯

The same animals are found in different continents. ◯

Britain has a similar climate to Iceland. ◯

Magnetic clues left in the rocks can track the movement of plates. ◯

(d) At first, many scientists did not accept the theory of continental drift. Why was this? [2]

....

....

(e) Mountains are thought to form as a result of tectonic plate movement. Explain how this happens. [2]

....

....

....

....

(f) Limestone is a sedimentary rock found in the Yorkshire Dales. When the limestone was studied by geologists they found fossils of fish, fragments of shells and water ripple marks in the rock. What does this evidence tell us about how the limestone was formed?

✏ *The quality of written communication will be assessed in your answer to this question.* [6]

....

....

....

....

....

....

....

....

[Total: .... / 56]

1. Five students watch their teacher demonstrate the reactions of lithium, sodium and potassium with water. They talk about what they see.

Joe
The sodium floated on the surface of the water.

James
The alkali metals seem to be getting more reactive as you go down the group.

Zoe
Sodium and potassium melt during the reaction with water but lithium does not.

Caroline
A flammable gas is produced during the reaction of alkali metals with water. A different colour flame can be seen for each different metal.

Richard
I think that caesium will explode when it is dropped into water.

(a) Which student is making a prediction rather than an observation? [1]

....

(b) Which student has identified a trend using observations from the experiment? [1]

....

(c) What gas is Caroline talking about? [1]

....

(d) James says that he has seen the reaction of caesium with water on a television programme. Is this a reliable source of information about this reaction? Explain your answer. [1]

....

....

....

2. **(a)** Complete the following table. [4]

	Mass	Charge	Where in the Atom is it Found?
Proton			In the nucleus
Electron	Approx. 0	Negative	Orbiting the nucleus
Neutron	1		

(b) What is the overall electrical charge on an atom? Explain your answer. [2]

....

....

....

(c) Complete the statement below about how many electrons fit into each electron shell. [3]

Up to .... electrons fit into the first shell; up to .... fit

into the second shell; up to .... fit into the third shell.

(d) Work out the electron configurations of the following elements, writing them with numbers to show the number of electrons in each shell. For example, boron has two electrons in its first shell and three in its second shell so it is written 2.3.

(i) Carbon (6 electrons): .... [1]

(ii) Chlorine (17 electrons): .... [1]

(iii) Sodium (11 electrons): .... [1]

(iv) Potassium (19 electrons): .... [1]

(e) What is the link between the electron configuration of an element and its group number? [1]

....

....

(f) What is the link between the electron configuration of an element and its period number? [1]

....

....

(g) An atom has four electrons in its third shell. What element is it? [1]

....

3. **(a)** Complete this paragraph. [3]

When atoms of an element are given lots of energy, for example, by heating them, they give off light

of a particular .... For example, sodium compounds always give off orange

light, as seen in many street lamps. This light can be analysed using a technique called

.... which helps chemists to identify the elements in stars in outer space.

This technique can be used to produce a line .... which is specific to that

element.

(b) Describe how to perform a flame test to distinguish between lithium chloride, sodium chloride and potassium chloride. You do not need to know the colours produced by these compounds.

✐ *The quality of written communication will be assessed in your answer to this question.* [6]

....

....

....

....

....

....

....

....

C4 Chemical Patterns

4. (a) Draw straight lines to show the correct meaning of each of the hazard symbols. [3]

Hazard symbol	Meaning
	Harmful
	Flammable
	Corrosive
	Oxidising agent

(b) Describe a precaution you would take when working with a flammable chemical. [1]

....

(c) Describe two precautions you would take when working with a harmful chemical. [2]

....

....

5. (a) Write down the symbols of four elements in Group 1. [1]

....

(b) What name is given to elements in Group 1? [1]

....

(c) Why are the Group 1 elements stored under oil? [1]

....

(d) Use your understanding of trends in the periodic table to complete the following table. Make sensible estimates where necessary. [3]

Element	Melting Point (K)	Boiling Point (K)	Formula of Chloride
Lithium	453		LiCl
Sodium	370	1156	
Potassium		1032	KCl

(e) Describe what you would **see** when a piece of sodium is put into a large bowl of cold water.   [2]

(f) (i) Write a word equation for the reaction between lithium and water.   [2]

(ii) Write a word equation for the reaction between sodium and chlorine.   [2]

(g) What happens to the reactivity of the Group 1 elements as you go down the group?   [1]

(h) Make a prediction about how caesium would react with water.   [1]

(i) Estimate the melting point of rubidium, in Kelvin.   [1]

K

6. This question is about the Group 7 elements.

(a) What name is given to the elements in Group 7? Put a tick (✓) in the box next to the correct answer.   [1]

The halogens ⬭

The noble gases ⬭

The transition metals ⬭

The salts ⬭

(b) The formula of chlorine is Cl_2. Which of the diagrams shows a chlorine molecule? Put a ring around the correct answer.   [1]

A   B   C   D

(c) Complete the following table. Make sensible estimates where necessary. [4]

Element	Formula	Appearance at Room Temperature (colour and state)	Melting Point (K)	Boiling Point (K)
Chlorine	Cl_2			239
Bromine		Orange/brown liquid, evaporates easily	266	332
Iodine	I_2	Grey solid, sublimes to purple vapour	387	

(d) Alex heats a small piece of lithium metal and places it into a gas jar full of chlorine gas. A reaction occurs that releases heat and light energy. A single product is made, which is a white solid salt. Write a word equation for the reaction that happens. [2]

(e) When a piece of lithium is placed into a gas jar of bromine gas, a similar reaction occurs and a different white solid salt is made. Would this reaction be faster or slower than when Alex performed the experiment with lithium and chlorine? Explain your answer. [2]

(f) Jess suggests to Alex that they could investigate the reactivity of halogens by seeing which halogens displace other halogens from solutions of their salts. Jess and Alex perform a series of experiments in which they bubble halogen gases through a solution of different potassium halide salts. They record their observations in a table which is shown below.

Element	Potassium Chlorine Solution	Potassium Bromide Solution	Potassium Iodide Solution
Chlorine	No reaction seen	Solution turns brown	Solution turns brown
Bromine	No reaction seen	No reaction seen	Solution turns brown
Iodine	No reaction seen	No reaction seen	No reaction seen

(i) Complete the following word equation. [2]

Chlorine + Potassium bromide $\longrightarrow$ .... + ...

(ii) Which is the most reactive halogen in this experiment? Put a (ring) around the correct answer. [1]

Chlorine   **Bromine**   **Iodine**

7. The table below shows some information about the electron configurations of some atoms and the ions that they form.

Element	Group Number	Number of Electrons in Atom	Electron Configuration of Atom	Electron Configuration of Ion	Charge on Ion
Lithium	1	3	2.1	2	+1
Sodium	1	11		2.8	+1
Potassium	1	19	2.8.8.1	2.8.8	+1
Magnesium	2	12	2.8.2	2.8	+2
Calcium	2	20	2.8.8.2	2.8.8	+2
Fluorine	7	9	2.7	2.8	−1
Chlorine	7	17	2.8.7	2.8.8	−1
Oxygen	6	8	2.6	2.8	−2

(a) How many electrons does an atom of fluorine have in its outer shell? [1]

....

(b) State the electron configuration of a sodium atom. [1]

....

(c) Strontium is an element in Group 2.

   (i) Suggest how many electrons strontium has in the outer shell of its atoms. [1]

....

   (ii) Explain your answer to part (i). [1]

....

(d) From the table, name a metal and a non-metal which form ions that have the same electron configuration. [1]

.... and ....

(e) Sulfur is a non-metal element in Group 6 and aluminium is a metal element in Group 3. Suggest what the charge will be on a sulfide ion and an aluminium ion. Explain your answer.

🖉 *The quality of written communication will be assessed in your answer to this question.* [6]

8. This question is about the periodic table.

(a) Which scientists were involved in developing the periodic table? Put ticks (✓) in the boxes next to the **three** correct answers. [3]

Plato ☐   Einstein ☐   Mendeleev ☐

Döbereiner ☐   Newlands ☐   Darwin ☐

(b) The diagram shows a simplified version of the periodic table.

							H										He
Li	Be											B	C	N	O	F	Ne
Na	Mg											Al	Si	P	S	Cl	Ar
K	Ca	Sc	Ti	V	Cr	Mn	Fe	Co	Ni	Cu	Zn	Ga	Ge	As	Se	Br	Kr
Rb	Sr	Y	Zr	Nb	Mo	Tc	Ru	Rh	Pd	Ag	Cd	In	Sn	Sb	Te	I	Xe
Cs	Ba	La*	Hf	Ta	W	Re	Os	Ir	Pt	Au	Hg	Tl	Pb	Bi	Po	At	Rn
Fr	Ra	Ac*	Rf	Db	Sg	Bh	Hs	Mt	Ds	Rg							

(i) What is a horizontal row in the periodic table called? [1]

(ii) What is the name given to the elements in the shaded area? [1]

(c) Draw straight lines to show the correct name for Groups 1, 7 and 0. [3]

Group   **Name**

| Group 1 |

| Group 7 |

| Group 0 |

| Halogens |

| Alkali metals |

| Noble gases |

| Alkaline earth metals |

9. **(a)** Describe how the ions are arranged in an ionic solid. You can answer the question using a diagram. [2]

(b) Describe what happens to the ions when an ionic solid is melted or dissolved. [1]

(c) Explain why ionic compounds do not conduct electricity when they are solid but do conduct electricity when they are molten or dissolved. [2]

(d) Using the diagram, explain what happens when lithium atoms form ionic bonds with fluorine atoms. Using ideas about stable electron configurations, explain why lithium and fluorine bond in this way.

✎ *The quality of written communication will be assessed in your answer to this question.* [6]

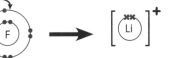

(e) Draw a dot-cross diagram similar to the one in part **(d)** to show ionic bonding between magnesium and oxygen. Remember that the metal atoms lose all their outer shell electrons and the non-metal atoms gain enough electrons to fill their outer shell. [2]

[Total: .... / 95]

Higher Tier

10. Use the periodic table on page 97 to help you to answer this question. Complete the table by working out the missing numbers of protons, electrons and neutrons in the following elements. [4]

Element	Number of Protons	Number of Electrons	Number of Neutrons
Lithium	3	3	4
Fluorine		9	
Aluminium	13	13	
Phosphorus	15		16

11. When potassium reacts with water, potassium hydroxide (KOH) and hydrogen gas are produced. Write a balanced symbol equation to show this. Include state symbols. [3]

12. **(a)** Explain why all Group 1 elements have similar chemical properties. [2]

(b) Explain why potassium is more reactive than sodium. [2]

13. State and explain the trend in reactivity in the halogens. [3]

14. (a) Looking at the diagrams, how many sodium ions and chloride ions would be needed to form a neutral compound of sodium chloride? Put a tick (✓) in the box next to the correct answer. [1]

One of each (NaCl) ☐

Two sodium ions and one chloride ion (Na_2Cl) ☐

One sodium ion and two chloride ions ($NaCl_2$) ☐

(b) If magnesium atoms form stable Mg^{2+} ions and oxygen atoms form stable O^{2-} ions, what will be the formulae of the following compounds?

(i) Magnesium oxide [1]

(ii) Magnesium chloride [1]

(iii) Sodium oxide [1]

(c) Given that the formula of an oxide of iron is Fe_2O_3 and the charge on an oxide ion is O^{2-}, work out the charge on the iron ion in this compound. [1]

(d) Strontium oxide has the formula SrO. What is the charge on the strontium ion? Explain your answer using ideas about the periodic table and electron configurations.

✎ *The quality of written communication will be assessed in your answer to this question.* [6]

[Total: ____ / 25]

C5 Chemicals of the Natural Environment

1. **(a)** Draw straight lines to show the correct definitions of atmosphere, lithosphere and hydrosphere. [2]

Word	Definition
Atmosphere	The Earth's crust and the solid outer part of the mantle
Lithosphere	The mixture of gases that surrounds the Earth
Hydrosphere	The Earth's oceans, lakes, aquifers, seas and rivers

(b) Complete the following table to show the amount of each gas in clean, dry atmospheric air. [4]

Gas	Formula	Percentage in Atmosphere
Nitrogen	N_2	78
Oxygen	O_2 ✓	68 x 21
Carbon dioxide	CO_2 ✓	0.04
Argon (and other gases)	Ar	The rest

gasse.

(c) Complete the following paragraph. Use words from this list. [5]

carbon dioxide   **electricity**   **heat**
nitrogen   **sound**   **strong**   **weak**

The atmosphere is made from a mixture of gases. Some are elements, including oxygen, argon

and __nitrogen__ ✓. Other gases are compounds, including __carbon dioxide__. These

substances all have low melting and boiling points because they are made from small molecules

with very __weak__ ✓ forces of attraction between the molecules. Most of the gases in the

atmosphere are made from molecules but argon is made from single atoms. Atoms in molecules

are joined by covalent bonds. These bonds are very __strong__ ✓. Molecular substances do

not conduct __electricity__ because their molecules are not charged. ✓

2. The table below shows data on seven different chemicals. Some of these are found in the atmosphere, some are found in the hydrosphere and some are found in the lithosphere.

Substance	Melting Point (°C)	Boiling Point (°C)	State at Room Temperature	Does it Conduct as a Solid?	Does it Conduct as a Liquid or Solution?
A	801	1413	Solid	No	Yes
B	0	100	Liquid	No	No
C	-78	-78	Gas	No	No
D	1650	2230	Solid	No	No
E	2072	2977	Solid	No	Yes
F	-210	-196	Gas	No	No
G	1064	2856	Solid	Yes	Yes

(a) Which of the substances is a metal? [1]

G ✓

(b) Which **two** substances are found in the atmosphere? [2]

F and C ✓ ✓

(c) Which of the substances is water? [1]

B ✓

(d) Which **two** substances are ionic? [2]

✗ Ionic

and

(e) Sometimes when a solid is heated, instead of melting it undergoes a process called **sublimation** in which the solid turns straight into a gas without forming a liquid first.

(i) Suggest which substance from the table does this. [1]

A ✗ C

(ii) Explain your answer to part **(i)**. [1]

because its got such a low melting & boiling point

(f) Silicon dioxide is the main compound in sand. Silicon dioxide has a giant covalent structure, similar to diamond. Its properties are similar to diamond as well. Suggest which of the substances is silicon dioxide. [1]

high melting point X. D

3. **(a)** What is an ion? [1]

a particle atom with a negative or positive charge

(b) Look at the diagram of part of a crystal of an ionic compound.

Key:

● Sodium ion

○ Chloride ion

a lattice

(i) Describe how the ions are arranged. [1]

the Sodium ions are in a row inbetween + chloride ions which are also in a row

(ii) What holds the ions together? [1]

the attraction between negative and positive ions

(c) Describe and explain the typical properties of ionic compounds.

🖉 _The quality of written communication will be assessed in your answer to this question._ [6]

+2

4. James is investigating a compound called zinc chloride.

(a) This is the container that contains the zinc chloride.

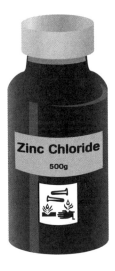

(i) What does the hazard symbol on the label mean? [1]

_____

(ii) Suggest one safety precaution that James should follow when using zinc chloride. [1]

_____

James sets up the apparatus in the diagram below.

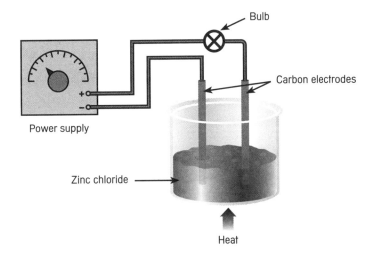

When James switches on the power supply, the bulb does not light at first. However, as he heats the zinc chloride, the bulb lights. James asks his friends to explain what he has seen.

Matthew
The liquid is conducting because it contains a metal.

Sarah
The zinc ions and the chloride ions are now free to move.

Deborah
Carbon conducts electricity so the bulb lights.

Martin
Hot substances conduct electricity better than cold substances.

(b) Which of James' friends has correctly explained why the bulb lights? [1]

....

(c) James continues to heat the zinc chloride in order to keep it molten. He leaves the power supply turned on. After a while, James notices a smell coming from the experiment. It smells of swimming pools and household bleach.

(i) What is the gas that James can smell? [1]

....

(ii) At which electrode will this gas be produced? Put a ring around the correct answer. [1]

Positive anode   Negative cathode

(d) Gill performs a similar experiment but she uses lead bromide instead of zinc chloride. Complete the table to suggest what is produced at each electrode. [2]

	Positive Anode	Negative Cathode
Gill's observations	Brown gas	Bead of molten metal in bottom of electrolyte
Element produced		

5. This question is about some of the gases that are present in the atmosphere.

(a) Draw straight lines to join the name of the gas to its formula and to the correct structure. One has been done for you. [4]

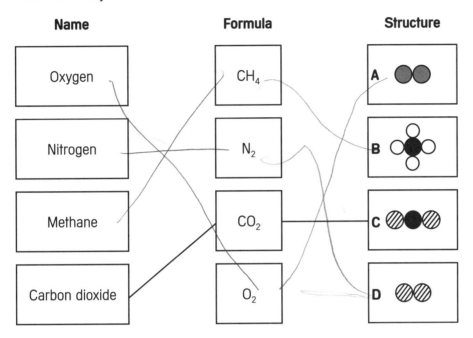

Name   **Formula**   **Structure**

Oxygen   CH$_4$

Nitrogen   N$_2$

Methane   CO$_2$

Carbon dioxide   O$_2$

(b) Here are some statements about the atmosphere. Put a tick (✓) in the correct box to show whether each statement is **true** or **false**. [3]

	true	false
The atmosphere contains mainly ionic substances.	✓	
The most abundant gas in the atmosphere is nitrogen.	✓	
The amount of carbon dioxide in the atmosphere is less than 1%.	✓	

6. **(a)** Complete the following paragraph. Use words from this list. [4]

    silicon   oxygen   graphite   aluminium   crust

The lithosphere is the outer part of the Earth. It is made from the ___crust___ and the solid,

outermost part of the mantle. The lithosphere is made from a mixture of minerals. Two pure forms

(allotropes) of carbon can be found in the lithosphere. They are diamond and ___graphite___.

Other elements that are very common in the lithosphere are ___silicon___,

___aluminium___ and oxygen. Much of the silicon and aluminium present in the lithosphere is

chemically bonded to ___oxygen___.

(b) The diagrams show two pure forms of carbon. Label them with their correct names. [2]

(i) _dimond_ ✓

(ii) _graphite_

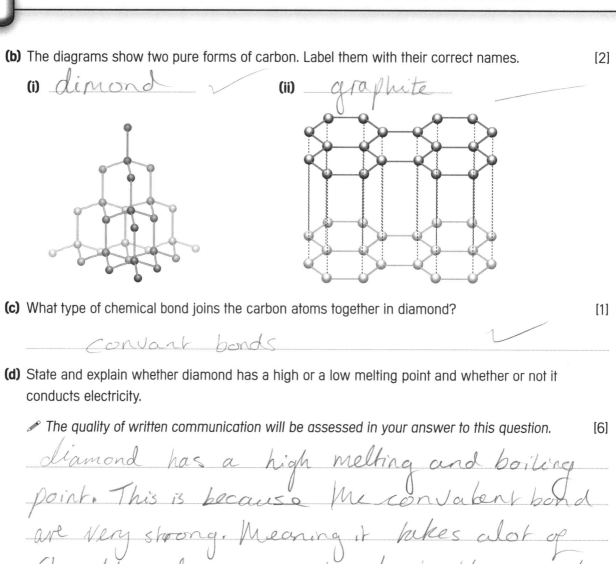

(c) What type of chemical bond joins the carbon atoms together in diamond? [1]

convant bonds ✓

(d) State and explain whether diamond has a high or a low melting point and whether or not it conducts electricity.

🖉 *The quality of written communication will be assessed in your answer to this question.* [6]

diamond has a high melting and boiling point. This is because the convalent bond are very strong. Meaning it takes alot of strenght and energy to brake them apart. Diamond also don't conduct electrihiy this is because there are no free electrons elechons.

(e) Describe how the structure of graphite is different from the structure of diamond. [2]

graphite has layers unlike diamond these layers have weak intermolecular forces alowing them to move.

OCR Twenty First Century GCSE Chemistry A Workbook Answers

Answering Quality of Written Communication Questions

A number of the questions in your examinations will include an assessment of the quality of your written communication (QWC). These questions are worth a maximum of 6 marks and are indicated by a pencil icon (✏).

Your answers to these questions will be marked according to...
- the level of your understanding of the relevant science
- how well you structure your answer
- the style of your writing, including the quality of your punctuation, grammar and spelling.

QWC questions will be marked using a 'Levels of Response' mark scheme. The examiner will decide whether your answer is in the top level, middle level or bottom level. The expected quality of written communication is different in the three levels and it will always be considered at the same time as looking at the scientific information in your answer:
- To achieve Level 3 (which is the top level and is worth 5–6 marks), your answer should contain relevant science, and be organised and presented in a structured and coherent manner. You should use scientific terms appropriately and your spelling, punctuation and grammar should have very few errors.
- For Level 2 (worth 3–4 marks), there may be more errors in your spelling, punctuation and grammar, and your answer will miss some of the things expected at Level 3.

- For Level 1 (worth 1–2 marks), your answer may be written using simplistic language. You will have included some relevant science, but the quality of your written communication may have limited how well the examiner can understand your answer. This could be due to lots of errors in spelling, punctuation and grammar, misuse of scientific terms or a poor structure.
- An answer given Level 0 may contain insufficient or irrelevant science, and will not be given any marks.

You will be awarded the higher or lower mark within a particular level depending on the quality of the science and the quality of the written communication in your answer.

Even if the quality of your written communication is perfect, the level you are awarded will be limited if you show little understanding of the relevant science, and you will be given Level 0 if you show no relevant scientific understanding at all.

To help you understand the criteria above, three specimen answers are provided to the first QWC question in this workbook. The first is a model answer worth 6 marks, the second answer would be worth 4 marks and the third answer worth 2 marks. The three exemplar answers are differentiated by their scientific content and use of scientific terminology. Model answers worth 6 marks are provided to all other QWC questions to help you aspire to the best possible marks.

Module C1: Air Quality
(Pages 3–13)

1. (a) A compound that contains only carbon and hydrogen.
    (b) Combustion **and** Oxidation **should be ticked**.
    (c)

    [1 for a correctly drawn CO₂ molecule; 1 for a correctly drawn H₂O molecule; 1 for showing one CO₂ molecule and two H₂O molecules]
    (d) There is a limited oxygen supply so carbon particulates and carbon monoxide may be produced.
    (e) **Any four from:** Fossil fuel sources will eventually run out so we need an alternative to power our cars; To reduce the atmospheric pollution caused by the combustion engine; To reduce the overall production of CO₂, which is a greenhouse gas; To improve the environment, e.g. reduce the amount of damage done to buildings by carbon particulates and acid rain; To help reach the Government's CO₂ reduction targets

2. (a) (i) cooled; condensed [Both needed for 1 mark.]
        (ii) photosynthesis; dissolving
        (iii) photosynthesis
    (b) Oxygen 21%; Nitrogen 78% [Both needed for 1 mark.]
    (c) **This is a model answer which would score full marks:**
    Changes in the composition of today's atmosphere resulting from human activity include the burning of fossil fuels in power stations and the combustion engine. When a fossil fuel burns, carbon dioxide and water vapour are released into the atmosphere. Many types of fossil fuel contain sulfur, which burns to produce sulfur dioxide.
    Deforestation is another example of how human activity is leading to increased levels of carbon dioxide in the atmosphere. Trees remove carbon dioxide by photosynthesis, thus lowering the levels. When trees are cut down they are

sometimes burned as fuel, which adds more carbon dioxide to the atmosphere.
The occurrence of volcanic eruptions is an example of how natural causes are also changing the composition of today's atmosphere. Large volumes of volcanic ash and gases such as carbon dioxide, sulfur dioxide and water vapour enter the atmosphere.
This answer would score 4 marks: Fossil fuels are burned in power stations and car engines. Carbon dioxide is made when this happens. If too much is burned, then lots of carbon dioxide will go into the atmosphere. Other gases are also made in the reaction, e.g. sulfur dioxide. When a volcano erupts it releases lots of gases, such as carbon dioxide, and volcanic ash into the atmosphere. It is a natural process that changes the composition.
This answer would score 2 marks: Humans burn fuels that put pollution into the air. Volcanoes cause pollution when they erupt because lots of ash and other stuff get blown into the air. So the amount of gas in the air will change.

3. (a) **Any suitable answer, e.g.** Generally, the sales of hay fever products increased when the pollen count increased and decreased when the pollen count decreased [1]. The sales peaked at the end of June after the pollen count had been at its highest, but in April, July and August sales did not increase as significantly as the pollen count [1]. The evidence is not conclusive because there are lots of variables such as temperature, humidity and other pollutants [1].
    (b) When pollen was stuck to the skin of volunteers, some volunteers had an allergic reaction [1]. The results show that people with a pollen allergy also suffered from hay fever. Those that did not have a pollen allergy did not suffer from hay fever [1].
    (c) Other scientists would study the data and repeat the skin tests [1]. The fact that the same results were always produced would prove that they were reliable [1].

(d) (i) That although nitrogen oxides can increase the chance of an asthma attack, it is not the only cause.

(ii) What factors cause asthma; What factors make asthma worse

4. (a) Always driving to the shops **and** Buying a car with a bigger engine **should be ticked**.

(b) (i) $2CO + O_2 \longrightarrow 2CO_2$
[1 for correct formulae; 1 for balancing correctly]

(ii) $2NO + 2CO \longrightarrow N_2 + 2CO_2$
[1 for correct formulae; 1 for balancing correctly]

(c) Fitting a filter system **and** Using hydroelectricity to power it **should be ticked**.

(d) (i) This is a model answer which would score full marks:
On a national level, new legislation was put into place. Legal limits have been set for vehicle exhaust emissions, which are enforced by the statutory MOT tests. This could have an impact on the local economy because, for example, garages would have to spend money updating their MOT testing systems. Also, catalytic converters have been made compulsory on new cars. This could have an impact on the local economy because new cars would need the latest technologies fitted, which may be more expensive.
There are schemes in place to help and encourage people to insulate their homes. These will lead to lower energy use and more local work. Local councils have taken measures such as introducing doorstep collections of paper, bottles, metals and plastics for recycling. This could have an impact on the local economy because it may create more jobs. Local councils are also providing more regular bus services and introducing park-and-ride schemes. Again, these measures could create more local jobs.

(ii) Any suitable answer, e.g. Different countries may take different action due to their specific circumstances **[1]**. For example, a mountainous country may invest in renewable energy such as hydroelectric power. A flat country may encourage people to cycle by developing a network of cycle paths around its cities **[1]**.

(e) Any suitable answer, e.g. Individuals can recycle paper, bottles, metals, plastics and textiles. This helps to conserve natural resources and also saves energy **[1]**. People can turn off electrical appliances in their home, such as the TV, rather than leaving them on standby. This uses less energy and therefore reduces the demand for energy from power stations, which in turn reduces air pollution **[1]**.

5. (a) (i) Any one from: Carbon dioxide comes from burning fossil fuels in power stations; Carbon dioxide comes from burning fossil fuels in the combustion engine.

(ii) Nitrogen monoxide is created because of the high temperatures in the combustion engine.

(iii) Sulfur dioxide comes from burning coal and other fossil fuels in power stations and combustion engines.

(iv) Carbon particulates come from the incomplete combustion of coal / fossil fuels.

(b)

Name	Formula	Molecule
Carbon dioxide	CO_2	
Nitrogen monoxide	NO	
Water	H_2O	
Sulfur dioxide	SO_2	

(c) Lines should be drawn from Carbon dioxide **to** Used by plants during photosynthesis; **from** Sulfur dioxide **to** Reacts with water to form acid rain; **from** Carbon particulates **to** Deposited on buildings **and from** Nitrogen oxides **to** Reacts with water to form acid rain. **[1 for each correct line.]**

(d) (i) To make sure that the carbon monoxide levels do not get too high

(ii) 5.2(ppm); 5.9(ppm) **[Both needed for 1 mark.]**

6. (a) The early atmosphere contained large amounts of water, carbon dioxide and ammonia **[1]**. Today's atmosphere contains large amounts of nitrogen, oxygen and a little carbon dioxide **[1]**.

(b) As green plants started to grow the amount of carbon dioxide went down **[1]** and the amount of oxygen went up **[1]**. This is due to the fact that, during photosynthesis, plants take in carbon dioxide and give out oxygen **[1]**.

(c) Any suitable answer, e.g. Scientists are worried that the composition of the atmosphere is changing due to human activity **[1]**. This in turn could have a massive impact on the environment, ultimately leading to climate change **[1]**. If scientists collect enough data to prove their theory, they will be able to put pressure on governments to make changes **[1]**. For example, if the levels of carbon dioxide are significantly higher in city centres, there is an argument for introducing congestion controls **[1]**.

7. (a) Variables (i.e. factors that change) affect concentrations, e.g. volume of traffic, weather conditions **[1]**; Accuracy of measuring equipment **[1]**; User's skill in using the measuring equipment and in recording the data accurately **[1]**

(b) 0.3(ppm); 3.5(ppm) **[Both needed for 1 mark.]**

(c) Any three from: To find the best estimate of the true value; To identify outliers; To allow discarding of outliers; To ensure that the results are reliable

(d) 0.3(ppm)

(e) Mean = Sum of all values ÷ Number of values
Mean for town centre = $(2.5 + 3.0 + 3.5) ÷ 3 = 3$(ppm)
The outlier has not been used in the calculation.
[1 for correct working but wrong answer; 1 for excluding outlier]
Mean for country park = $(0.2 + 0.1 + 0.1 + 0.2) ÷ 4$
$= 0.15$(ppm) **[1]**

(f) The concentration of sulfur particles is significantly higher in the town centre **[1]**. The data supports the theory because there are more vehicles and buildings in the town centre than in the countryside **[1]**.

(g) Yes, because the difference between the mean values is a lot greater than the range of each set of data **[1]**. If the difference between the mean values had been smaller than the range there would not have been a real difference. The result would have been insignificant and the data would not support the theory **[1]**.

8. (a) (i) The nitrogen and oxygen in the air react together **[1]** because of the high temperatures in the engines **[1]**.

(ii) Nitrogen monoxide **[1]**

[1 for correctly drawn NO molecules; 1 for balancing correctly]

(iii) Oxidation **should be ticked**.

(b) A mixture of nitrogen oxides **[1]**; NO and NO_2 **[1]**

(c) Nitrogen oxides are greenhouse gases **[1]** and cause acid rain **[1]**.

(d) Nitrogen; Carbon dioxide **[1]**

[1 for correctly drawn molecules; 1 for balancing correctly]

9. (a) Coal contains sulfur atoms **[1]**. During combustion the sulfur reacts with oxygen to form sulfur dioxide **[1]**.

(b) absorbed

(c) Sulfur dioxide is an acidic oxide **[1]** and when dissolved in water it forms acid rain **[1]**.

Module C2: Material Choices
(Pages 14–21)

1. (a)

Material	Natural Resources	Chemical Synthesis
Nylon		✓
Wood	✓	
PVC		✓
Wool	✓	

(b) **Any suitable answer, e.g.**

Material	Properties	Uses
Nylon	Lightweight Stretchy Strong Waterproof	**Any one from:** **Clothing** **Climbing ropes**
Wood	Quite a good insulator of heat Hard and rigid Waterproof	**Any one from:** **Fences** **Furniture**
PVC	High tensile strength Tough and durable Not very stretchy Waterproof	**Window frames**
Wool	Medium strength Good insulator of heat Stretchy Adsorbs water	**Any one from:** **Clothing** **Carpets**

[1 for each material]

(c) (i) To ensure that the results were reliable **[1]**; To find the best estimate of the true value to work out the mean value **[1]**; To identify any outliers **[1]**

(ii) 615.9(kN); 617.5(kN) **[Both needed for 1 mark.]**

2. (a) Fractional distillation **should be ticked**.

(b) Carbon; Hydrogen **[Both needed for 1 mark; no marks if any others listed.]**

(c) The strength of the forces between the hydrocarbon molecules increases as the length of the molecule increases **[1]**. More energy is needed to break the forces between the molecules in the liquid form to make a gas **[1]**. So, molecules with different lengths will evaporate at different temperatures, allowing the separation of the different hydrocarbons **[1]**.

3. (a) Gwyneth; Jonathan

(b) **This is a model answer which would score full marks:**
Suncream contains nanoparticles of titanium dioxide which are very good at absorbing ultraviolet radiation, making the sunscreen more effective.
Many leading manufacturers of sports equipment have started adding nanoscale silicon dioxide crystals to tennis rackets. The resulting polymer gives better performance without changing the weight. The tennis rackets with silicon nanoparticles are stronger and more efficient.
[Other examples of products that use nanoparticles to change the properties of materials used to make the products are acceptable.]

(c) Nanotechnology is still in the early stages of development **[1]**. Some products are being put on the market before they have been fully tested **[1]**. It may take many years for any harmful health effects to become apparent and be linked to nanotechnology **[1]**.

4. (a) **This is a model answer which would score full marks:**
All three materials are strong enough for the children to sit on, so the class didn't think that strength was an important factor.
Polypropene is cheaper than both wood and iron, however, so they will be able to buy more chairs with their money.
Polypropene also has a low density so it will be easy to move the chairs around, whereas iron and wood may both be too heavy for the children to move on their own.

(b) Polypropene is made from a non-renewable material **and** Polypropene is non-biodegradable **should be ticked**.

(c) In strong winds a polypropene chair could be blown away but an iron one would not be **[1]**. This is because iron has a much higher density than polypropene **[1]**.

5. (a) C_2H_3Cl

(b) Monomers **should be ticked**.

(c) Small molecules **[1]** (called monomers) are joined together to make a long molecule / chain **[1]** called a polymer.

(d) **Diagram C should be ticked**.

(e) A plasticizer is a small molecule which sits between the polymer chains **[1]**. This forces the chains to be further apart **[1]**, which weakens the forces between the chains **[1]**, allowing the molecules to move more freely.

6. (a) **Diagram A should be ticked**.

(b) Cross-linking **should be ticked**.

(c) Vulcanised rubber is used to make car tyres because it has a higher tensile strength **[1]** and is harder **[1]** than naturally occurring rubber. This is because during vulcanisation strong cross-links are formed between the polymer chains **[1]**, so that they are no longer able to move **[1]** (see diagram B).

7. (a) (i) **B – Buckminster fullerene should be ringed**.

(ii) **Any suitable answer, e.g.** They have a much larger surface area to volume ratio **[1]** than larger particles of the same materials, which means they can be used to change existing properties **[1]**. For example, they can make polymers stronger **[1]**.

(b) (i) **Any two from:** Unreactive; Shiny; Does not react with water

(ii) **Any two from:** Antibiotics are more effective as they are easier to get into the body; Silver can be hard to remove from around the wound when the patient is better; If silver doesn't dissolve it will not get to the main problem area; Silver is expensive

(iii) **This is a model answer which would score full marks:**
When silver is applied directly to the wound, the particles are too large to be dissolved and absorbed directly into the body. The healing process is very slow. Nanoscale silver particles are very much smaller and have different properties due to the much larger surface area to volume ratio. Unlike the larger particles, the nanoscale particles can be absorbed directly into the body, making the healing process much quicker.

(iv) **Any suitable answer, e.g.** Inform the public that there are regulations for the development of new products **[1]**. Inform the public that reports by scientific advisors suggest that most nanotechnologies fit within the regulations **[1]**. Include a warning label saying that the long-term effects of exposure to a particular material are not known **[1]**.

Module C3: Chemicals in Our Lives: Risks and Benefits
(Pages 22–32)

1. (a) The Earth's crust is made up of large pieces of rocks called tectonic plates **[1]**. These move slowly across the Earth's surface **[1]**.

(b) **Any two from:** Africa and South America look like two pieces of a jigsaw; The same fossils have been found in different continents; There are magnetic clues left in the rocks that can track the movement of plates; The same rocks are found in different continents; Rocks in Britain have formed in different climatic regions.

(c) (i) **Mountains form where the plates meet. This should be clearly marked on the diagram.**

(ii) When two continental plates move towards each other **[1]**, they are pushed upwards **[1]**, forming mountains.

(d) **This is a model answer which would score full marks:**
As rocks are weathered small fragments are broken off. The fragments are broken down further as they are transported to different places by the process of erosion. Eventually the sediments enter the sea. Over the years, layers of sediments build up. Eventually the increased pressure causes minerals to be formed as the water is squeezed out. Eventually sandstone is formed. The process of sedimentation takes millions of years.

2. (a)

B	A	D	E	C

[1 for each correctly placed up to a maximum of 4.]
   (b) **Any three from:** Creates an ugly landscape; Produces noise and air pollution from the machinery and increased traffic; Destroys natural habitats; Creates dips on the surface where the ground is sinking
   (c) (i) Electrolysis **should be ringed.**
      (ii) Hydrogen, Chlorine **and** Sodium hydroxide **should be ticked. [All three needed for 1 mark.]**
      (iii) Chlorine is a toxic gas and could damage wildlife if there was a leak **[1]**.
         Hydrogen is explosive and if set alight would do extensive damage to natural habitats **[1]**.
         Sodium hydroxide is corrosive and will burn living tissue, which would damage wildlife if there was a leak **[1]**.
         If other chemicals were ticked in part (ii), the following answers are acceptable:
         Hydrochloric acid is either corrosive or an irritant depending on concentration, so will harm living tissue **[1]**.
         Sodium chlorate is corrosive, so can cause burns to living tissue and gives off a toxic gas if in contact with an acid **[1]**.
         There are no real environmental concerns associated with water **[1]**.
         [To gain each mark, the environmental effect of each product must be given.]

3. (a) Too much salt can lead to headaches **should be ticked.**
   (b) To improve the taste **and** To make the food last longer **should be ticked. [Both needed for 1 mark.]**
   (c) **Any two from:** Salt is a preservative **[1]** that allows processed foods to be kept longer. Food with less salt would have a shorter shelf life. This would mean that the processed foods would have to be replaced more regularly, which would cost the company more money **[1]**. Food with less salt may not taste as nice **[1]**.
   (d) So that the public know what is in the food products **[1]** and so that they can calculate, for example, how much salt or how many calories they are eating each day **[1]**.
   (e) They decide what must be put on food labels **[1]**; They carry out tests to ensure that the food is safe to eat **[1]**; They monitor the food industry to make sure that food companies are operating within the law **[1]**.

4. (a) To encourage a reduction in waste **[1]**; To increase awareness of the environmental impact **[1]**
   (b) Making the material from raw materials, Manufacture, Use, Disposal **should be ticked.**
   (c) (i) Reusable nappies are better **[1]**. They produce a lot less waste than disposable nappies **[1]**. During manufacture they use less energy and raw materials **[1]** and less water is wasted **[1]**.
      (ii) **Either disposable or reusable nappies will gain a mark but the choice must be supported by a suitable reason, e.g.** Most parents will choose disposable nappies because they are much more convenient to use; Most parents will choose reusable nappies because they are much better for the environment.

5. (a) Increases **should be ticked.**
   (b) Too much salt can increase the chance of a heart attack **should be ticked.**

(c) (i) $1.1 + 0.2 + 1.8 + 0.7 + 0.2 = 4.0(g)$
   (ii) $6.0 - 4.0 = 2.0(g)$
   (iii) Abigail should have the beef burger and salad **[1]** because this would mean her salt intake for the day is still within the RDA **[1]**, whereas the other meal would take her above the RDA.
(d) **This is a model answer which would score full marks:**
Salt is a preservative so the food will keep for longer. It can also add flavour to poor quality ingredients. Processed food is cheaper to buy than fresh ingredients and contains more salt. If less salt was used, the profits the restaurants make may decrease. The restaurants could increase their prices but this might reduce the number of customers.

6. (a) Burnt wood **and** Stale urine **should be ticked.**
   (b) (i) To neutralise acid soil
      (ii) To bind natural dyes to clothes
      (iii) To make glass
   (c) (i) Hydrogen chloride will form acid rain **[1]**, which damages plants and buildings **[1]**.
         Heaps of waste materials create an ugly landscape / destroy natural habitats **[1]**.
         Hydrogen sulfide will poison living things **[1]**.
      (ii) Pollution caused by a chemical can sometimes be addressed by a chemical reaction **[1]**. When a chemical reacts with something else, different compounds are made. These compounds will have different properties which may be harmless to the environment **[1]**.
   (d) (i) Sodium chloride
      (ii) Sulfuric acid; Water **[Both needed for 1 mark.]**
      (iii) Nitric acid; Carbon dioxide **[Both needed for 1 mark.]**
   (e) Calcium carbonate will react with the acid rain **[1]** to produce a salt, water and carbon dioxide gas **[1 for products as words or equation for reaction]**. As a result, the limestone will wear away more quickly **[1]**.

7. (a) To provide data about how many deaths from cancer there are that are a result of causes other than pollution, so that comparisons can be made
   (b) (i) It varied between about 50 and 60 deaths per hundred thousand people.
      (ii) It varied between about 90 and 105 deaths per hundred thousand people.
   (c) The study shows that there is a link between access to treated drinking water and the number of deaths from cancer **[1]**. Recommend further studies are carried out to confirm the results **[1]** and water treatment centres are built in the polluted and most polluted areas **[1]**.
   (d) **This is a model answer which would score full marks:**
In the previously polluted and most polluted areas, the number of deaths from cancer would be expected to have dropped to about the same as the control areas. However, the death rate in the control area may also have dropped due to other improvements such as greater access to medicines. The general health would be expected to have improved as a result of adding chlorine to the water, as chlorine kills many of the microorganisms that are responsible for diseases (such as typhoid).

8. (a) **Any one from:** A solid crust formed; Mountains formed
   (b) Large slabs of rock that make up the Earth's crust and upper mantle
   (c) Africa and South America look like two pieces of a jigsaw; The same fossils are found in different continents **and** Magnetic clues left in the rocks can track the movement of plates **should be ticked.**
   (d) **Any two from:** They had not seen all the evidence; At the time it seemed a ridiculous theory because no one could actually see the plates moving; They couldn't explain why the plates would move; It went against the accepted theories of the day; It disagreed with biblical theories because this would make the Earth millions of years old.

(e) Any suitable answer, e.g. When two plates collide as a result of moving towards each other [1], huge pressures cause the rocks to fold and buckle [1], resulting in the formation of mountains; When an oceanic plate and a continental plate collide [1] and the denser continental plate is forced down under the oceanic one [1], new mountains are formed.

(f) This is a model answer which would score full marks: Sedimentary rocks are made up from a range of different types of sediment, shown by the presence of fossils and shells. The types of fossil found in the different layers of rock would tell scientists about processes that took place a very long time ago. The Yorkshire Dales was once part of the marine environment and the sediments, including fish and broken shells, built up on the ocean bed. The ripple marks found in the rock show that the water was still there during the final stages of sedimentation.

Module C4: Chemical Patterns (Pages 33–43)

1. (a) Richard
(b) James
(c) Hydrogen
(d) Any one from: Yes, because the reaction has been filmed and is therefore reliable evidence; No, because the reaction might have been faked.

2. (a)

	Mass	Charge	Where in the Atom is it Found?
Proton	1	**Positive**	In the nucleus
Electron	Approx. 0	Negative	Orbiting the nucleus
Neutron	1	**No charge**	**In the nucleus**

(b) Neutral [1] because every atom has the same number of positive protons and negative electrons [1].
(c) two; eight; eight ['18' is also acceptable.]
(d) (i) 2.4
(ii) 2.8.7
(iii) 2.8.1
(iv) 2.8.8.1
(e) The group number is the number of electrons in the outer shell.
(f) The period number is the number of full or partially-filled electron shells.
(g) Silicon

3. (a) colour / frequency / wavelength [1]; spectroscopy [1]; spectrum [1]
(b) This is a model answer which would score full marks: Take a nichrome wire loop. Clean it by dipping in acid and then heating it in a blue Bunsen flame. Use the loop to pick up a few crystals of the solid to be tested and place it into the blue Bunsen flame. Record the colour of the flame and compare it with known samples or a reliable reference such as a textbook. [An answer which states using a splint instead of a wire loop would also be acceptable.]

4. (a) Lines should be drawn from the first symbol to Corrosive; from the second symbol to Flammable; from the third symbol to Oxidising agent and from the fourth symbol to Harmful. [1 for each correct line up to a maximum of 3.]
(b) Any one from: Turn off Bunsen burner; Keep away from hot objects; Keep away from sources of ignition
(c) Any two from: Wear gloves; Wear goggles; Wear a lab coat

5. (a) Any four from: Li; Na; K; Rb; Cs; Fr [Four needed for 1 mark.]
(b) Alkali metals
(c) To prevent them from reacting with (oxygen or moisture in) the air.

(d)

Element	Melting Point (K)	Boiling Point (K)	Formula of Chloride
Lithium	453	**Any answer greater than 1250**	LiCl
Sodium	370	1156	**NaCl**
Potassium	**Any answer less than 350**	1032	KCl

(e) Any two from: The sodium floats; It fizzes; It moves around on the surface; It gets smaller.
(f) (i) Lithium + Water $\longrightarrow$ Lithium hydroxide + Hydrogen [1 for correct reactants; 1 for correct products]
(ii) Sodium + Chlorine $\longrightarrow$ Sodium chloride [1 for correct reactants; 1 for correct product, correctly spelt]
(g) It increases
(h) Any one from: It will react violently; It will explode; The reaction will be faster than with potassium.
(i) Any answer less than 300K.

6. (a) The halogens should be ticked.
(b) Diagram C should be ringed.
(c)

Element	Formula	Appearance at Room Temperature (colour and state)	Melting Point (K)	Boiling Point (K)
Chlorine	Cl_2	**Green gas**	**Any answer between 100 and 200**	239
Bromine	**Br_2**	Orange / brown liquid, evaporates easily	266	332
Iodine	I_2	Grey solid, sublimes to purple vapour	387	**Any answer between 387 and 400**

(d) Lithium + Chlorine $\longrightarrow$ Lithium chloride [1 for correct reactants; 1 for correct product]
(e) Slower [1] because bromine is less reactive than chlorine [1].
(f) (i) Potassium chloride; Bromine
(ii) Chlorine should be ringed.

7. (a) Seven
(b) 2.8.1
(c) (i) 2
(ii) Any one from: All elements in Group 2 have two electrons in their outer shell; It will follow the pattern seen in magnesium and calcium atoms in the table; The group number is the same as the number of electrons in the outer shell of an atom.
(d) Any one pair (both required for 1 mark) from: Sodium and fluorine; Sodium and oxygen; Magnesium and fluorine; Calcium and chlorine; Potassium and chlorine; Magnesium and oxygen
(e) This is a model answer which would score full marks: Sulfur is in Group 6 and therefore has six electrons in its outer shell. It will gain two electrons to achieve a full outer shell, which is a stable electron configuration. Gaining two electrons will give the sulfide ion a charge of 2– (S^{2-}). Aluminium is in Group 3 and therefore has three electrons in its outer shell. It will lose three electrons to achieve an empty (or full) outer shell. Losing three electrons will cause the aluminium ion to have a charge of 3+ (Al^{3+}).

8. **(a)** Döbereiner, Newlands **and** Mendeleev **should be ticked**.
   (b) (i) A period
   (ii) Any one from: The transition metals; The transition elements
   (c) Lines should be drawn from Group 1 **to** Alkali metals; **from** Group 7 **to** Halogens **and from** Group 0 **to** Noble gases.
   [1 for each correct line.]

9. **(a)** Oppositely charged ions **[1]** are arranged in a regular lattice **[1]**. **2 marks can also be obtained by a diagram, e.g.:**

   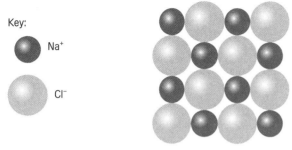

   Key:
   - Na⁺
   - Cl⁻

   (b) The ions can move freely.
   (c) In a solid, the ions are locked in place **[1]**. In a liquid or solution, the ions are free to move and conduct electricity **[1]**.
   (d) This is a model answer which would score full marks:
   One electron from the outer shell of a lithium atom will be transferred to a fluorine atom. This leaves the lithium as a stable positive ion with an empty outer shell and the fluorine as a stable negative ion with a full outer shell. The opposite charges on the lithium (Li^+) and the fluoride (F^-) ions cause them to be strongly attracted and form an ionic lattice.
   (e)

   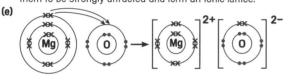

   [1 for correct electron configurations of ions and 1 for correct charges]

10.

Element	Number of Protons	Number of Electrons	Number of Neutrons
Lithium	3	3	4
Fluorine	**9**	9	**10**
Aluminium	13	13	**14**
Phosphorus	15	**15**	16

11. $2K(s) + 2H_2O(l) \rightarrow 2KOH(aq) + H_2(g)$ **[1 for correct formulae; 1 for balancing correctly; 1 for correct state symbols]**

12. **(a)** All the Group 1 elements have one electron in their outer shell **[1]**. All the Group 1 elements need to lose one electron to become stable **[1]**.
   (b) Potassium's outer electron is further from its nucleus **[1]** so it is lost more easily **[1]**. **[No marks for 'the outer electron is lost faster'.]**

13. Reactivity decreases as you go down the group **[1]** because the atom gains an electron less easily **[1]**. This is due to the electron going into a shell that is further from the nucleus / the electron being attracted less strongly **[1]**.

14. **(a)** One of each (NaCl) **should be ticked**.
   (b) (i) MgO
   (ii) MgCl$_2$
   (iii) Na$_2$O
   (c) Fe^{3+} / positive 3
   (d) This is a model answer which would score full marks:
   The strontium ion will have a charge of 2+ (Sr^{2+}). This can

be explained in two ways. First, strontium is in Group 2 so its atoms have two electrons in their outer shell. These two outer electrons will be lost during ionic bonding so the ion will have a charge of 2+. Second, the formula of strontium oxide, SrO, shows that one strontium ion is needed for each oxide ion. Oxygen is in Group 6 so its atoms have six electrons in their outer shell and would need to gain two electrons to become stable ions. The charge on an oxide ion is therefore 2– (O^{2-}) so the charge on a strontium ion would need to be Sr^{2+}.

Module C5: Chemicals of the Natural Environment (Pages 44–58)

1. **(a) Lines should be drawn from** Atmosphere **to** The mixture of gases that surrounds the Earth; **from** Lithosphere **to** The Earth's crust and the solid outer part of the mantle **and from** Hydrosphere **to** The Earth's oceans, lakes, aquifers, seas and rivers. **[1 for each correct line up to a maximum of 2.]**
   (b)

Gas	Formula	Percentage in Atmosphere
Nitrogen	N$_2$	78
Oxygen	**O$_2$**	**21**
Carbon dioxide	**CO$_2$**	0.04
Argon (and other gases)	**Ar**	The rest

   (c) nitrogen; carbon dioxide; weak; strong; electricity

2. **(a)** G
   (b) C; F
   (c) B
   (d) A; E
   (e) (i) C
   (ii) Because it melts and boils at the same temperature (i.e. instantaneously)
   (f) D

3. **(a)** An atom or group of atoms with an electrical charge.
   (b) (i) Any one from: In a regular arrangement; In a lattice
   (ii) Any one from: Electrostatic forces; Attraction between oppositely charged ions
   (c) This is a model answer which would score full marks:
   One typical property of ionic compounds is that they have high melting points. This is because the oppositely charged ions are held together in a lattice by very strong electrostatic forces of attraction which require a lot of energy to break. Another property is that ionic compounds do not conduct electricity when they are solid because the ions are fixed in place. However, when the compound is melted or dissolved, the ions are free to move and so the substance can conduct electricity.

4. **(a) (i)** Corrosive
   (ii) Any one from: Wear gloves; Wear goggles
   (b) Sarah
   (c) (i) Chlorine
   (ii) Positive anode **should be ringed**.
   (d)

	Positive Anode	Negative Cathode
Gill's observations	Brown gas	Bead of molten metal in bottom of electrolyte
Element produced	**Bromine**	**Lead**

5. **(a) Lines should be drawn from** Oxygen **to** O$_2$ **and then to** Diagram D; **from** Nitrogen **to** N$_2$ **and then to** Diagram A **and from** Methane **to** CH$_4$ **and then to** Diagram B.
   [1 for each correct line linking names and formulae up to a maximum of 2; 1 for each correct line linking formulae and diagrams up to a maximum of 2.]

(b) The atmosphere contains mainly ionic substances: false; The most abundant gas in the atmosphere is nitrogen: true; The amount of carbon dioxide in the atmosphere is less than 1%: true

6. **(a)** crust; graphite; aluminium; silicon **[these two in any order]**; oxygen **[1 for each correct up to a maximum of 4.]**
   (b) (i) Diamond
   (ii) Graphite
   (c) Covalent bond
   (d) This is a model answer which would score full marks:
   The melting point of diamond is very high because it has a giant covalent structure. Each carbon atom is bonded to four other carbon atoms by strong covalent bonds which require a lot of energy to break. There are no delocalised electrons or other charged particles (such as ions) that are free to move, so diamond does not conduct electricity.
   (e) Any two from: Carbon atoms in graphite are bonded in layers; Each carbon atom is bonded to three others, not four as in diamond; There are weak forces between the layers; There are delocalised electrons in graphite.
   (f) Any suitable answer, e.g. Graphite has many **[1]** strong / covalent **[1]** bonds which require a lot of energy **[1]** to break; In graphite each carbon atom is bonded to three other carbon atoms **[1]** by strong / covalent **[1]** bonds which require a lot of energy **[1]** to break.
   (g) Graphite has delocalised electrons **[1]** which are able to move between the layers **[1]** and carry charge **[1]**.

7. **(a)** High melting point **[1]** because **[any one from]** strong / covalent bonds between atoms **[1]** require a lot of energy to break **[1]** like diamond **[1]**.
   (b) Very hard **[1]** because **[any one from]** strong / covalent bonds between atoms **[1]** require a lot of energy to break **[1]** like diamond **[1]**.
   (c) Will not conduct electricity **[1]** because there are no electrons or ions **[1]** that are able to move **[1]**.

8. oxygen; reduction; redox; electrolysis; gold **[1 for each correct up to a maximum of 4.]**

9. **(a) (i)** 56
   (ii) 63.5
   (iii) 16
   (b) (i) 79.5
   (ii) 232

10. **(a) [1 for each correct up to a maximum of 3.]**
    (i) Carbon anode
    (ii) Electrolyte
    (iii) Aluminium siphoned off
    (iv) Cathode
    (b) The ions become free to move through the electrolyte.
    (c) The Al^{3+} ions move towards the cathode **[1]** because they are attracted to the opposite / negative charge **[1]**.
    (d) The O^{2-} ions move towards the anode **[1]** because they are attracted to the opposite / positive charge **[1]**.

11. **Lines should be drawn from** Copper used for electrical wiring **to** Good electrical conductor **and then to** Delocalised electrons are free to move.
    Lines should be drawn from Aluminium used for saucepans **to** High melting point **and then to** Strong bonds between metal ions take a lot of energy to overcome.
    Lines should be drawn from Steel used for car body panels **to** Malleable and strong **and then to** Strong bonds between metal ions can re-form in a new shape.
    A line should be drawn from Good conductor of heat **to** Close-packed metal ions transfer vibrations effectively.
    [1 for each correct line linking boxes in the first column with boxes in the second column up to a maximum of 2; 1 for each correct line linking boxes in the second column with boxes in the third column up to a maximum of 3.]

12. **(a) Lines should be drawn from** Reusing metals **to** Very little environmental impact; **from** Recycling metals **to** Uses a lot less energy than mining the ore and extracting the metal **and from** Throwing away metals **to** Landfill sites destroy natural habitats and heavy metals can pollute groundwater. **[1 for each correct line up to a maximum of 2.]**
    (b) Any three from: Noise pollution; Increased traffic; Pollution from transport; Dust; Loss of natural habitats; Deforestation; Carbon dioxide emissions from machinery

13. **(a)** The nuclei are both attracted to the electrons **[1]** that are shared in the covalent bond **[1]**.
    (b) They all have a full outer shell.
    (c)

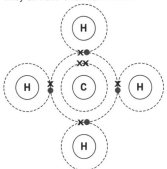

    [1 for four pairs of electrons in the outer shell of the carbon atom; 1 for positioning these four pairs of electrons so that they overlap the shell of each of the four hydrogen atoms.]

14. **(a)** Add sodium hydroxide solution **[1]**. A light blue precipitate identifies copper ions **[1]**.
    $Cu^{2+} + 2OH^- \longrightarrow Cu(OH)_2$ **[1 for correct formulae and charges; 1 for balancing correctly]**
    (b) Carbonate ions are not present; Sulfate ions are present
    (c) This is a model answer which would score full marks:
    Zoe should test to see if the metal ion is iron(II) or iron(III) by adding sodium hydroxide solution. If iron(II) ions are present, Zoe will see a green precipitate. If iron(III) ions are present, Zoe will see a red-brown precipitate. Zoe can distinguish between the chloride, bromide and iodide ions by adding dilute nitric acid and then silver nitrate solution to a new sample of the water. A white precipitate indicates chloride ions are present, a cream precipitate indicates bromide ions are present and a yellow precipitate indicates iodide ions are present.

15. **(a)** Calcium carbonate
    (b) Silver nitrate **[1]** and sodium chloride / sodium carbonate **[1]**
    (c) (i) (White) precipitate
    (ii) Calcium nitrate + Sodium carbonate $\longrightarrow$ <u>Calcium carbonate</u> + Sodium nitrate **[1 for correct products; 1 for correct underlining]**
    (d) $AgNO_3(aq) + NaCl(aq) \longrightarrow AgCl(s) + NaNO_3(aq)$ **[1 for correct formulae of reactants; 1 for correct formulae of products; 1 for correct state symbols]**

16. **(a)** 160
    (b) 112(g)
    (c) 102
    (d) 102g of Al_2O_3 contains 54g of aluminium **[1]** so 51g contains 27(g) **[1]**.
    (e) (i) Any three from: Negative oxide ions **[1]** are attracted because they have opposite charge **[1]**. They lose electrons **[1]** to form oxygen atoms / molecules **[1]**.
    $2O^{2-} \longrightarrow O_2 + 4e^-$ **[1 for correct half equation]**
    (ii) Any three from: Positive aluminium ions **[1]** are attracted because they have opposite charge **[1]**. They gain electrons **[1]** to form aluminium atoms **[1]**.
    $Al^{3+} + 3e^- \longrightarrow Al$ **[1 for correct half equation]**

17. **(a) (i) Any one from:** Magnesium ion; Positive ion **[No marks for 'Magnesium' or 'Magnesium atom'.]**
    (ii) Delocalised electron

(b) Electrostatic force
(c) The delocalised electrons **[1]** are able to move **[1]** and so carry the charge.
(d) External forces cause the layers of metal ions to move by sliding over each other **[1]**. When the metal ions are displaced, they are held in their new positions by strong forces of attraction from the delocalised electrons **[1]**.

Module C6: Chemical Synthesis
(Pages 59–72)

1. (a) (i) **Lines should be drawn from** Sulfuric acid **to** Copper sulfate **and from** Copper sulfate **to** Copper oxide. **Lines should be drawn from** Hydrochloric acid **to** Magnesium chloride **and from** Magnesium chloride **to** Magnesium oxide.
        [1 for each correct line.]
    (ii) Harmful
    (iii) **Any one from:** Wear goggles; Wear gloves
    (b) **Symbol E should be ticked.**

2. (a) Aluminium sulfate; Water
    (b) Limewater **should be ticked**.
    (c) Unreacted aluminium oxide
    (d) **This is a model answer which would score full marks:** Lizzy should filter the mixture to remove the insoluble, unreacted aluminium oxide. She should then heat the solution of aluminium sulfate to evaporate some of the water and leave the mixture to cool to allow crystals to form. She should then place the crystals in an oven or desiccator to dry them.

3. (a) less than; greater than; citric; sulfuric; gas
    (b) (i) Salt; Hydrogen
        (ii) Salt; Water
        (iii) Salt; Water
        (iv) Salt; Water; Carbon dioxide
    (c) (i) H^+
        (ii) OH^-
        (iii) $H^+ + OH^- \longrightarrow H_2O$

4. (a) **This is a model answer which would score full marks:** An exothermic reaction releases energy into the surroundings, usually as heat. An endothermic reaction absorbs energy from the surroundings. You can classify a reaction as exothermic or endothermic by recording the temperature change of the surroundings. For example, burning is an exothermic reaction because if you burn a fuel below a beaker of water, the temperature of the water increases.
    (b) **Any one from:** The reaction mixture getting too hot; Possibility of an explosion; Melting the equipment

5. risk; temperature; purified; crystallise; desiccator

6. (a) (i) **Any one from:** 12; 13; 14
        (ii) The universal indicator in the acid has gone from red to green **[1]**, which indicates that the acid has been neutralised **[1]**.
    (b) (i) **Any one from:** Use the same amount of acid; Use acid from the same bottle; Use acid of the same concentration.
            Any one from: Add one tablet to each beaker; Add the same mass of tablet to each beaker.
        (ii) Peptocool **[1]** because it has increased the pH more than the other two **[1]**.
    (c) Calcium chloride + Carbon dioxide + Water **[All three required for 1 mark.]**
    (d) Magnesium + Hydrochloric acid ⟶ Magnesium chloride **[1]** + Hydrogen **[1]**
        Magnesium carbonate + Hydrochloric acid ⟶ Magnesium chloride + Carbon dioxide **[1]** + Water **[1]**

Hydrogen is flammable but carbon dioxide is harmless in your stomach **[1]**.
[The mark for magnesium chloride can be awarded to either but not both word equations.]

7. (a) RFM of $CaCO_3$ = 100
        RFM of CaO = 56
        So 200g of $CaCO_3$ will produce 112(g) of CaO
        [1 for correct working but wrong answer]
    (b) (i) Nitric acid
        (ii) $\frac{8}{12} \times 100 = 66.7(\%)$
            [1 for correct working but wrong answer]

8. (a) (i) Pipette
        (ii) Conical flask
        (iii) Burette
    (b) conical flask; burette; drop; neutralised; distilled
    (c) $\frac{20 \times 0.15}{25} = 0.12(mol/dm^3)$
        [1 for correct working but wrong answer]

9. (a) **Any one from:** The amount of product made per unit time; The amount of reactant used per unit time.
        ['The speed at which a reaction occurs' would also gain 1 mark.]
    (b) **Any two from:** To maximise the amount of product made in a certain time; To make product more quickly; To slow down unwanted reactions
    (c) Smelling the reaction mixture **should be ticked**.

10. (a) Increase the concentration; Increase the temperature; Grind lumps of the reactant into a powder / Increase the surface area of the reactant; Add a catalyst
        ['Increase pressure' would also be acceptable.]
    (b) They are used up in the reaction: false; They are always solids: false; They are chemically unchanged at the end of the reaction: true; They reduce the amount of energy needed by the reactants: true
    (c) collision; energy; activation
    (d) **This is a model answer which would score full marks:** Increasing the concentration of an aqueous solution will speed up a chemical reaction because reactant particles will be more crowded, so collisions will be more frequent. Grinding lumps of a solid reactant into a powder will increase its surface area, exposing more reactant particles and so, again, collisions will be more frequent.

11. (a)

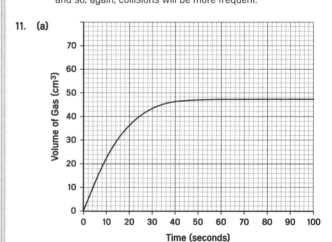

[1 for plotting points correctly; 1 for a smooth curve of best fit.]
    (b) 50 (seconds)
    (c) 47(cm^3)

(d) Any suitable answer, e.g.

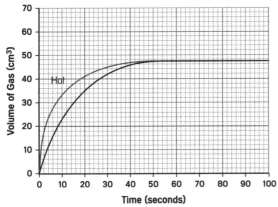

[1 for the line being steeper at start; 1 for the line finishing at same height]

(e) Any suitable answer, e.g.

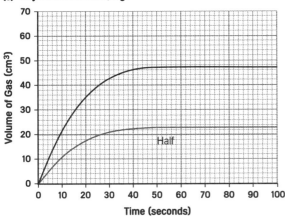

[1 for the line finishing at half the height of the original line.]

12. (a) Any two from: There would be a fast / violent / dangerous reaction; The potassium would float; The potassium would fizz; There would be bubbles of gas / hydrogen produced; The potassium / hydrogen would catch fire.

(b) (i) $2KOH + H_2SO_4 \longrightarrow K_2SO_4 + 2H_2O$

(ii) Lines should be drawn from H^+ **to** Sulfuric acid **and from** Sulfuric acid **to** SO_4^{2-}.
Lines should be drawn from K^+ **to** Potassium hydroxide **and from** Potassium hydroxide **to** OH^-.
[1 for each correct line.]

(iii) The reaction is a neutralisation reaction: true; You can tell when the reaction has finished because it will stop fizzing: false; The ionic equation for this reaction is $H^+ + OH^- \longrightarrow H_2O$: true; All acids contain OH^- ions: false

13. Any suitable answer, e.g.

Endothermic   **Exothermic**

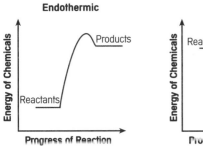 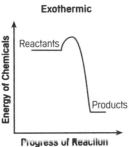

[1 for endothermic graph finishing higher than it starts and for exothermic graph finishing lower than it starts; 1 for correct placement of reactants and products labels on both graphs; 1 for both graphs rising before they fall.]

14. (a) $Fe_2O_3 + 2Al \longrightarrow 2Fe + Al_2O_3$ **[1 for correct formulae; 1 for balancing correctly]**

(b) (i) 160
(ii) 102

(c) 160g of Fe_2O_3 would require $2 \times 27g$ of Al = 54g of Al
So 16g of Fe_2O_3 would require 5.4(g) of Al
[1 for correct working but wrong answer]

(d) 160g of Fe_2O_3 should produce $2 \times 56g$ of Fe = 112g of Fe
So 16g of Fe_2O_3 should produce 11.2(g) of Fe
[1 for correct working but wrong answer]

15. (a) Any one from: The carbon dioxide has escaped; She cannot measure the mass of the carbon dioxide.

(b) 123.5

(c) 0.44(g)

(d) $(0.40 \div 0.57) \times 100 = 70(\%)$
[1 for correct working but wrong answer]

Module C7: Further Chemistry
(Pages 73–96)

1. (a) −COOH **should be ringed**.

(b) Any one from: CH_3COOH; CH_3CO_2H; $C_2H_4O_2$

(c) A molecule of methanoic acid is made up of three different types of atom **and** Carboxylic acids react with metals to produce a salt and hydrogen gas **should be ticked**.

(d) Water; Carbon dioxide **[Both needed for 1 mark.]**

(e) (i) Any two from: Food flavourings; Fragrances; Solvents
(ii) Ethanol; Water

2. (a) C_2H_4 **and** C_4H_{10} **should be ticked**.

(b) saturated, single **[Both needed for 1 mark.]**; less, unsaturated **[Both needed for 1 mark.]**; more, double **[Both needed for 1 mark.]**

(c) (i) C_2H_5OH
(ii) CH_4
(iii) C_3H_8
(iv) Any one from: HCO_2H; $HCOOH$; CH_2O_2

(d) Methane **[or any other hydrocarbon]**; Oxygen; Carbon dioxide; Water **[1 for naming a hydrocarbon; 1 for all the rest correct]**

3. (a) Food flavourings; Fuel **and** Adhesives **should be ticked**.

(b) Alcohols are less dense than water; It is the −OH group in a molecule of an alcohol that is attracted to a molecule of water; Carboxylic acids are responsible for the taste of rancid butter **and** Fats and oils are used by living organisms as an energy store **should be ticked**.

(c) (i) Polyunsaturated fats are fats that contain more than one [1] carbon−carbon double bond [1].
(ii) Any two from: Because the double bonds make them more reactive [1], so they are easier to break down [1]; Too many saturated fats can lead to an increase in cholesterol level [1].

4. (a) Food additives **and** Fragrances **should be ticked**.

(b)

C	A	E	D	B

[1 for each correctly placed up to a maximum of 3.]

(c) To protect people [1] and the environment [1] from danger

(d) This is a model answer which would score full marks:
The chemical is explosive and highly flammable, which means it will catch fire easily. It is also oxidising, which means it will provide oxygen that will allow other substances to burn more fiercely. The following safety precautions should be taken. A no-smoking rule must be imposed near the tanker and the tanker must carry a fire extinguisher and fire blanket. Also, the driver must be made fully aware of what the tanker is carrying and what to do in an emergency.

5. (a) Suncream D would not be approved [1] as it may irritate sensitive skin [1]. Suncream E would be approved [1] as it has the correct sun protection factor and does not cause any reaction with the skin [1].

(b) People may be angry, cross or annoyed [1] because suncream C has a sun protection factor lower than advertised [1], so people using it could get burned by the sun, increasing their risk of getting skin cancer [1].

6. (a) The Monsanto process [1] as it can use biomass, a renewable feedstock [1], or hydrogen, which can be taken from renewable feedstocks [1], and carbon monoxide, which is often a by-product of other reactions [1].
   (b) In the Monsanto process there is no waste [1]. All the atoms in the reactants are also in the product, ethanoic acid [1]. There is a lot of waste in the pre-1970s method; in fact 65% is waste [1]. **Any one from:** The manufacturers would have to find safe ways to dispose it; This amount of waste could lead to a lower profit margin.
   (c) The catalyst lowers the activation energy of the reaction **and** The catalyst speeds up the reaction without being chemically changed at the end of it **should be ticked**.
   (d) They wanted to find a more efficient catalyst [1]; A more efficient catalyst could speed up the reaction / A more efficient catalyst could enable the reaction to take place at even lower temperatures / They could make ethanoic acid at a lower cost / They could make a bigger profit [1].
   (e) **This is a model answer which would score full marks:**
   Yes I think it should be allowed. Countries should be allowed to choose what method they use. It would cost a lot of money to upgrade plants with new technology. There is still crude oil available as a feedstock and local supplies of crude oil may be cheaper and easier to obtain than biomass. Over the years, countries may develop ways of effectively dealing with the by-products.
   This is an alternative model answer which would also score full marks:
   No I do not think it should be allowed. The old technology is not very sustainable compared to the newer technology that is available. It relies on non-renewable feedstocks that will eventually be depleted. It also produces a lot of waste that could be avoided if the newer process was used. Companies need to invest in the future. A new plant will be more efficient as well as more environmentally friendly and, in the longer term, it will save the company money. Governments have a responsibility to reduce global carbon emissions.

7. (a) Citric acid, Methanoic acid **and** Butanoic acid **should be ticked**.
   (b) A weak acid is less reactive than hydrochloric acid **should be ticked**.
   (c) True [1]. The pH scale tells us how acidic a solution is by measuring the concentration of hydrogen ions in the solution [1], so the stronger the acid the more H^+ ions are released [1] and the lower the pH value [1].

8. (a) energy; endothermic; activation; less
   (b) Reaction A

9. (a) $\rightleftharpoons$
   (b) It reaches a dynamic equilibrium **should be ticked**.
   (c) Ammonia
   (d) (i) Nitrogen + Hydrogen $\rightleftharpoons$ Ammonia [1 for correct reactants and products; 1 for correct symbol]
       (ii) $N_2 + (3)H_2 \rightleftharpoons (2)NH_3$ [1 for correct formulae of reactants and products; 1 for correct symbol]
   (e) (i) natural gas
       (ii) nitrogen
       (iii) recycled
   (f) (i) It increases the yield.
       (ii) It decreases the yield.

10. (a) greater; recycling; decreasing; exothermic
    (b) Lightning [1]
    None or any one from: The enormous energy of lightning breaks the strong covalent bonds in the nitrogen molecules [1]. This enables nitrogen atoms to react with oxygen in the air [1], forming nitrogen oxides [1].

Any one from: Nitrifying bacteria; Nitrogen-fixing bacteria containing the enzyme nitrogenase
Any one or two from: These bacteria are found in root nodules [1] of leguminous plants [1] and they convert nitrogen into nitrates [1].
   (c) **Any one from:** It is an essential nutrient for plants; To increase soil fertility; To produce enough food to feed the world's population.

11. **This is a model answer which would score full marks:**
    Catalysts provide an alternative reaction pathway with a lower activation energy, so they speed up a reaction and can also allow it to happen at a lower temperature. This saves money and so allows a manufacturing company to maximise its profits. Enzymes usually work best at approximately 40°C, which is a very cheap temperature to maintain. Enzymes can also be produced by biotechnology, which might be cheaper than the catalysts currently used (transition metals, which can be expensive).

12. (a) **This is a model answer which would score full marks:**
    Qualitative methods usually detect the presence of a substance. For example, iron(II) ions can be identified by adding sodium hydroxide and observing a green precipitate. Chloride ions can be identified by adding nitric acid and then silver nitrate and observing a white precipitate. Quantitative methods usually involve measuring the amount of a substance in a sample, for example, by titration.
    [Other examples of qualitative and quantitative analysis are acceptable.]
    (b) To ensure that the results are valid / reliable / representative of the whole
    (c) Procedures that are followed by all scientists / everyone

13. (a) **Any one from:** Organic; Not water
    (b) **This is a model answer which would score full marks:**
    Use a piece of chromatography paper as the stationary phase and draw a pencil line across it, near the bottom. Place a spot of the substance to be tested on the line, alongside other substances which you suspect might be present in the unknown substance. Allow the spots to dry. Place the piece of paper in a beaker with a small amount of water in. Water is the mobile phase. The depth of the water should be lower than the pencil line. Over time, the water will rise up the chromatography paper and separate the mixture of substances. You can identify the substances present in the mixture by comparing them with the known substances or by calculating an R_f value.
    (c) **Any two from:** Faster runs; Greater movement of the mobile phase; A choice of different absorbencies for the stationary phase; Greater separation
    (d) A substance used to show the presence of colourless spots.
    (e) (i) Mystery compound: $4 \div 6 = 0.67$
            Cocaine: $2 \div 6 = 0.33$
            Heroin: $5 \div 6 = 0.83$
            Laundry powder: $4 \div 6 = 0.67$
        (ii) Laundry powder
    (f) It can be compared with a reference from another source, e.g. the Internet or a data book.

14. (a) mobile; stationary; heated; quickly; retention
    (b) (i) Seven
        (ii) 70 (seconds)
        (iii) Compound F
        (iv) Compound A
        (v) Compound G
        (vi) **Any one from:** No because there is no peak at 140 seconds; Possibly because the lack of a positive result may not mean a negative result / the athlete may be taking a different performance-enhancing drug from the one being tested for / a repeat test might be needed / more evidence is needed.

15. (a) **Lines should be drawn from** Pipette **to** Used to measure a specific volume of liquid which goes in the conical flask;

from Burette **to** Used to accurately measure the volume of the second reactant added; **from** White tile **to** Allows the colour change of the indicator to be seen easily **and from** Clamp and stand **to** Holds the burette securely and vertically. **[1 for each correct line up to a maximum of 3.]**

(b) **Any one from:** g/dm³; mol/dm³

(c) **Any one from:** To achieve concordant results; To improve or check reliability; To exclude outliers; To allow an average to be calculated

(d) pH meter

16. (a)
C	A	D	F	B	G	H	E

[1 for each correctly placed up to a maximum of 4.]

(b) (i)
	Start Volume (cm³)	End Volume (cm³)	Titre (cm³)
Rough	0.0	26.1	**26.1**
Titration 1	26.1	51.3	**25.2**
Titration 2	1.0	26.6	**25.6**
Titration 3	3.5	29.4	**25.9**

(ii) No **[1]** because he doesn't have results that are concordant / sufficiently close together **[1]**.

(c) (i)
	Start Volume (cm³)	End Volume (cm³)	Titre (cm³)
Rough	0.0	25.9	**25.9**
Titration 1	1.5	26.6	**25.1**
Titration 2	0.3	25.6	**25.3**
Titration 3	2.1	27.4	**25.3**

(ii) Correct selection of two concordant results: 25.3, 25.3 **[1]**
Average = (25.3 + 25.3) ÷ 2 = 25.3(cm³)
[1 for correct working; 1 for correct answer. Working must be shown.]

(iii) $\frac{25.3 \times 0.1}{25}$ = 0.1012(mol/dm³)
[1 for correct working but wrong answer. Answer rounded to 0.1 would also gain 2 marks.]

(d) $\frac{25 \times 1.5}{2 \times 30}$ = 0.625(mol/dm³)

[1 for correct working but wrong answer. Answer rounded to 0.6 would also gain 2 marks.]

17. (a) (i) A result that is unusual and falls far outside the range of the majority of the results.
(ii) No

(b) (11.4 + 11.8 + 10.9 + 11.4 + 11.1) ÷ 5 = 11.32(g/dm³)
[1 for correct working; 1 for correct answer. Working must be shown.]

(c) 10.9(g/dm³); 11.8(g/dm³) **[Both required for 1 mark.]**

(d) 0.9

(e) (0.9 ÷ 11.32) × 100 = 7.95(%) **[1 for correct working but wrong answer. An appropriately rounded answer, e.g. 8%, would also gain 2 marks.]**

18. (a)
B	C	A	D

[1 for each correctly placed up to a maximum of 2.]

(b) (i) Reflux
(ii) Purification

(c) (i) **Any two from:** Continuous boiling **[1]**. The liquid boils and as the vapours cool **[1]** they condense back to a liquid and fall back into the reaction vessel to boil again **[1]**.
(ii) Concentrated sulfuric acid acts as a catalyst **[1]** to speed up the reaction **[1]**.

(d) **Any two from:** The distillate is transferred to a separating funnel where a solution of sodium carbonate is added **[1]**.

The sodium carbonate reacts with any excess acid and extracts it into the aqueous phase **[1]**. The aqueous phase is then run off into a flask, leaving the ester in the funnel **[1]**.

(e) Anhydrous calcium chloride removes water molecules **[1]** by absorbing them. The solid calcium chloride is removed by filtration **[1]**.

19. (a) **Any suitable answer including any four points from:** Percentage yield tells us how efficient the reaction is **[1]**. It is a measure of how much product is 'lost' during a reaction **[1]**. Atom economy tells us how sustainable a reaction is **[1]**. It tells us how much waste there is **[1]**. For example, an atom economy of 100% means that all the reactant atoms end up in the product and there are no by-products **[1]**.

(b) (i) Relative formula mass of ethanoic acid
= 24 + 4 + 32 = 60
Relative formula mass of sodium ethanoate
= 24 + 3 + 23 + 32 = 82
The equation shows a 1:1 (or 2:2) ratio so the theoretical yield is $\frac{82}{60}$ × 30 = 41g

Percentage yield = $\frac{31}{41}$ × 100 = 75.6(%)
[1 for correct working but wrong answer]

(ii) **Any suitable answer including any three points from:** During the different stages of synthesis, some of the product or intermediate compounds may be 'lost' **[1]**. Some may be left on the side of the reaction vessel **[1]**, some could get spilt when being transferred to or from different pieces of equipment **[1]**. Also, another product could be made **[1]**.

(iii) Relative formula mass of useful product = 2 × 82 = 164
Relative formula mass of reactants
= 2 × 60 + (46 + 12 + 48) = 226
Atom economy = $\frac{164}{226}$ × 100 = 72.6(%)
[1 for correct working but wrong answer]

(iv) 100 − 72.6 = 27.4%

20. (a) −OH **should be ticked.**
(b) $C_2H_5OH(l) + 3O_2(g) \longrightarrow 3H_2O(g) + 2CO_2(g)$
[1 for the correct formulae; 1 for the correct state symbols; 1 for balancing correctly]
(c) Sodium would sink in the ethanol **[1]** and steadily give off hydrogen gas **[1]**.
(d) Sodium ethoxide
(e) (i) The sodium would float **[1]** and melt / move around on the surface / give off hydrogen rapidly **[1]**.
(ii) $2Na(s) + 2H_2O(l) \longrightarrow 2NaOH(aq) + H_2(g)$
[1 for correct formulae of reactants; 1 for correct formulae of products; 1 for balancing correctly; 1 for correct state symbols]

21.

[1 for the line for products lower than the line for reactants; 1 for Activation energy hump and label; 1 for Energy change / ΔH / Enthalpy change correctly labelled.]

22. (a) (i) Energy in = 436 + 151 = 587
Energy released = 2 × 298 = 596
Total energy change = 587 − 596 = -9(kJ/mol)
[1 for correct working but wrong answer]
(ii) Exothermic

(b) (i) Energy in = $(2 \times 436) + 496 = 1368$
Energy released = $4 \times 463 = 1852$
Total energy change = $1368 - 1852 = -484$(kJ/mol)
[1 for correct working but wrong answer]

(ii) Exothermic

23. (a) They are equal.

(b) This is a model answer which would score full marks:
Increasing the pressure increases the yield but it requires expensive equipment and the running costs are high due to the energy demands. The pressure chosen is a compromise between yield and cost. Increasing the temperature decreases the yield but increases the rate of reaction, so the temperature chosen is a compromise between rate and yield. A catalyst is used to speed up the reaction but it does not affect the yield.

24. (a) $10g \times 4 = 40$(g/dm³)
[1 for correct working but wrong answer]

(b) 60g in 1000cm³
So 6g in 100cm³
So 1.5g in 25cm³.
[1 for correct working but wrong answer. Alternative methods are acceptable.]

25. (a)

	Start Volume (cm³)	End Volume (cm³)	Titre (cm³)
Rough	0.0	16.0	**16.0**
Titration 1	0.6	15.2	**14.6**
Titration 2	1.9	16.8	**14.9**
Titration 3	4.5	19.5	**15.0**

(b) $(15.0 + 14.9) \div 2 = 14.95$(cm³)
[1 for correct working but wrong answer]

(c) 1 to 1 ratio of KOH to HNO_3 **[1]**
So Volume of KOH × Concentration of KOH
= Volume of HNO_3 × Concentration of HNO_3
Concentration of KOH = $(14.95 \times 1.0) \div 20$
= 0.7475(mol/dm³)
[1 for correct working but wrong answer. An appropriately rounded answer, e.g. 0.7, would also gain 2 marks]

(f) Explain why graphite has a very high melting point. [3]

because of its Giant convalent bond making it

(g) Graphite is very unusual in that it is one of a very small number of covalently bonded non-metal substances that can conduct electricity. Explain how it can do this. [3]

7. Here is a diagram of silicon dioxide.

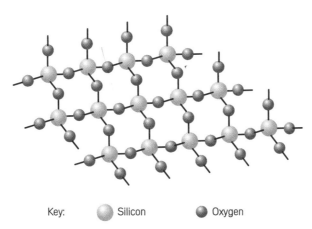

Key: ● Silicon ● Oxygen

Use your understanding of how bonding and structure determine the properties of a substance to predict and explain the following properties of silicon dioxide.

(a) Melting point: [2]

(b) Hardness: [2]

(c) Electrical conductivity: [3]

8. Complete the following paragraph using the words below. [4]

reduction   **oxygen**   **redox**   **electrolysis**   **gold**

The lithosphere contains many types of rock, including some that contain minerals from which metals can be economically extracted. These rocks are called ores. Some of the metals are very valuable so it is worth mining and purifying large quantities of ore to extract a small amount of metal. Many ores contain metal elements that are bonded to .... This must be removed in a process that is the opposite to oxidation, called .... Many less reactive metals can be reduced by heating them with carbon, which reacts with the oxygen and removes it. The carbon is therefore oxidised while the metal is reduced. When oxidation and reduction take place at the same time, we call the overall process .... More reactive metals must be reduced using a process called .... , in which electricity is used to split up a dissolved or molten ionic compound. The least reactive metals, such as .... , do not easily react with oxygen so they are found pure in the lithosphere.

9. **(a)** Use the periodic table on page 97 to write down the relative atomic masses of the following elements.

  (i) Iron: .... [1]

  (ii) Copper: .... [1]

  (iii) Oxygen: .... [1]

(b) Work out the relative formula mass of the following compounds.

  (i) CuO: .... [1]

  (ii) Fe_3O_4: .... [1]

10. Aluminium is extracted from aluminium oxide by electrolysis.

(a) Label the following diagram using the words below. [3]

Carbon anode   **Cathode**   **Electrolyte**   **Aluminium siphoned off**

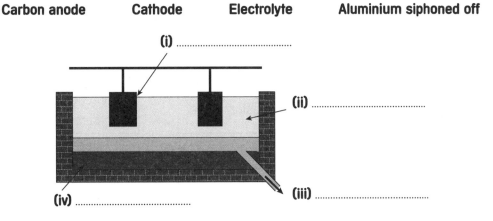

(i) ....

(ii) ....

(iii) ....

(iv) ....

(b) Describe what happens to the aluminium ions (Al^{3+}) and the oxide ions (O^{2-}) when the solid aluminium oxide dissolves into the electrolyte. [1]

....

....

(c) Describe and explain what happens to the aluminium ions during the electrolysis of molten aluminium oxide. [2]

....

....

....

(d) Describe and explain what happens to the oxide ions during the electrolysis of molten aluminium oxide. [2]

....

....

....

11. For each use of a metal, draw a line to the relevant property and another line from the property to the explanation of that property. One line has been drawn for you. [5]

Use	Property	Explanation
Copper used for electrical wiring	Malleable and strong	Close-packed metal ions transfer vibrations effectively
Aluminium used for saucepans	Good conductor of heat	Strong bonds between metal ions can re-form in a new shape
Steel used for car body panels	Good electrical conductor	Strong bonds between metal ions take a lot of energy to overcome
Titanium used for heat exchangers	High melting point	Delocalised electrons are free to move

12. (a) Draw lines to show the impact on the environment of each method of disposal. [2]

Method	Impact on environment
Reusing metals	Uses a lot less energy than mining the ore and extracting the metal
Recycling metals	Landfill sites destroy natural habitats and heavy metals can pollute groundwater
Throwing away metals	Very little environmental impact

(b) Give **three** environmental impacts of mining metals and metal ores. [3]

1. ....

2. ....

3. ....

[Total: .... / 98]

13. The dot-cross diagram shows the covalent bonding in water.

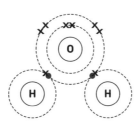

(a) The nuclei of the oxygen atom and both hydrogen atoms are positively charged. Why do they not repel each other and force the molecule apart? [2]

....

....

(b) Explain why all three atoms in the molecule of water are stable. [1]

....

(c) Draw a dot-cross diagram showing the covalent bonding in a molecule of methane (CH_4). [2]

14. You may find that the data sheet on page 98 helps you to answer this question.

Zoe works as a chemist at a water supply company. She tests the water regularly to ensure that it is safe for customers to drink.

(a) Copper ions are harmful to people. Describe the test that Zoe would perform to see if there are copper ions present in the water. Describe what the positive result would be. Use an ionic equation in your answer. [4]

....

....

....

(b) Zoe takes a sample of water and adds hydrochloric acid to it. Nothing happens. She then adds barium chloride to the sample and a white solid forms, which falls to the bottom of the test tube. What **two** conclusions can Zoe make about the ions present in this water sample? [2]

1. ....

2. ....

(c) The following week, Zoe hears that the water might have been contaminated with an iron compound. It is possible that the compound is one of the following:

Iron(II) chloride

Iron(II) bromide

Iron(II) iodide

Iron(III) chloride

Iron(III) bromide

Iron(III) iodide

Describe and justify two tests that Zoe should perform and how her results will confirm the compound present in the water.

✎ *The quality of written communication will be assessed in your answer to this question.* [6]

....

....

....

....

....

....

....

....

....

....

15. The tables below give information about the solubility of some substances. Use the data in the tables for this question.

Soluble in Water	
Sodium chloride	Sodium carbonate
Sodium nitrate	Calcium nitrate
Calcium chloride	Silver nitrate

Insoluble in Water
Calcium carbonate
Silver carbonate
Silver chloride

(a) When sodium carbonate solution is mixed with calcium chloride solution, a precipitate is formed. What is it? [1]

....

(b) Which two solutions could be mixed to form an insoluble precipitate containing silver ions? [2]

....

(c) What would you expect to see if calcium nitrate solution was mixed with sodium carbonate? Write a word equation and underline any precipitate that you would expect to see.

(i) Observation: .... [1]

(ii) Word equation: .... [2]

(d) Write a symbol equation, including state symbols, for the reaction between silver nitrate ($AgNO_3$) and sodium chloride solutions. [3]

....

16. **(a)** Work out the relative formula mass of Fe_2O_3. [1]

....

(b) What mass of iron could be extracted from 160g of Fe_2O_3? [1]

.... g

(c) Work out the relative formula mass of Al_2O_3. [1]

....

(d) What mass of aluminium could be extracted from 51g of Al_2O_3? [2]

....

.... g

(e) During the electrolysis of aluminium oxide, Al^{3+} ions and oxide ions (O^{2-}) are free to move in the electrolyte. State and explain which ions are attracted to each electrode and what happens to them, using ideas about electrons. Use half equations in your answer.

(i) Positive electrode (anode): _____ [4]

_____

_____

(ii) Negative electrode (cathode): _____ [4]

_____

_____

17. The diagram shows metallic bonding.

(a) Label the two different types of particle in the lattice structure. [2]

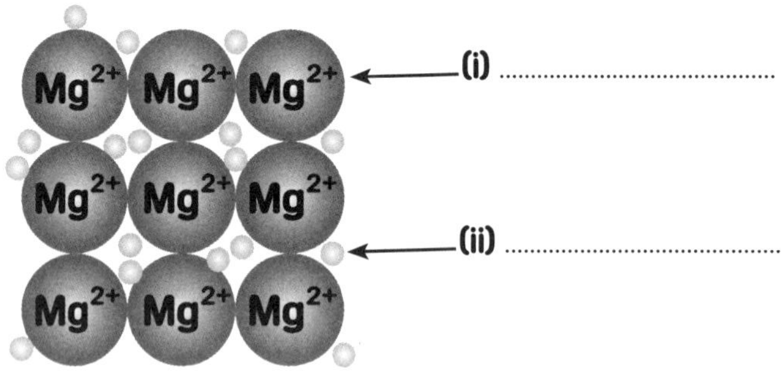

(b) What type of force holds together the oppositely charged particles in a metal? [1]

_____

(c) Explain how metals conduct electricity. [2]

_____

_____

(d) Explain how the structure and bonding in metals allows them to be malleable. [2]

_____

_____

_____

[Total: _____ / 46]

1. Joe decides he wants to make crystals of different salts to investigate their shapes and colours.

   (a) Two of the salts he wants to make are copper sulfate and magnesium chloride.

      (i) Draw lines to show which two reactants Joe should use to make each of these salts. [4]

Reactant	Product	Reactant
Nitric acid	Copper sulfate	Copper oxide
Hydrochloric acid	Magnesium chloride	Magnesium oxide
Sulfuric acid		Iron oxide

      (ii) Joe looks at the bottle of hydrochloric acid.

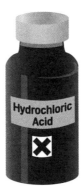

What does the symbol on the label mean? [1]

_____

      (iii) Suggest a safety precaution that Joe should observe when using hydrochloric acid. [1]

_____

   (b) Joe's teacher tells him that the solution of copper sulfate he has made is toxic. Which of the hazard symbol stickers should Joe put on the beaker containing his copper sulfate solution? Put a tick (✓) in the box next to the correct answer. [1]

 A 　　　　B

C 　　　　D

E

2. Lizzy decides to make some aluminium sulfate crystals. She reacts aluminium oxide with sulfuric acid.

(a) Complete the word equation for this reaction. [2]

Aluminium oxide + Sulfuric acid ⟶ .... + ...

(b) After the reaction, Lizzy tests the pH of the solution to make sure it is neutral. Which of the following would **not** be suitable for this purpose? Put a tick (✓) in the box next to the unsuitable method. [1]

Universal indicator ◯

Limewater ◯

pH probe ◯

(c) Lizzy notices some white solid in the bottom of the beaker which contains the neutral aluminium sulfate solution. Suggest what the insoluble white solid might be. [1]

....

(d) Lizzy wants to remove the unwanted white solid from the solution of aluminium sulfate and then make crystals of aluminium sulfate. Describe how she should do this. Include all the steps in the process and explain why each one is needed.

🖉 *The quality of written communication will be assessed in your answer to this question.* [6]

....

....

....

....

....

....

....

....

....

....

3. **(a)** Complete the following paragraph. Use words from this list. [5]

citric   **gas**   **greater than**   **less than**   **solid**   **sulfuric**

Acids and alkalis are measured on the pH scale, which is usually shown from pH 1 to 14. Acids

have pH values that are _____ 7, while alkalis have pH values that are

_____ 7. A solution with a pH of 7 is said to be neutral. Soluble metal

hydroxides are always alkalis. Some pure acids are solid, such as _____ acid,

while others are liquid, such as ethanoic, nitric and _____ acids. Hydrogen

chloride is an example of an acid that is a _____ at room temperature.

When an acid and an alkali react together, this is called a neutralisation reaction.

(b) Complete the general word equations below.

(i) Acid + Metal ➡ _____ + _____ [2]

(ii) Acid + Alkali ➡ _____ + _____ [2]

(iii) Acid + Metal oxide ➡ _____ + _____ [2]

(iv) Acid + Metal carbonate ➡ _____ + _____ + _____ [3]

(c) **(i)** Which ion is always present when an acid dissolves in water? Show the charge on the ion. [1]

_____

(ii) Which ion is present in all alkalis? Show the charge on the ion. [1]

_____

(iii) Write an ionic equation to show how water is made in an acid–alkali neutralisation reaction. [1]

_____

4. **(a)** Explain what is meant by the terms **exothermic** and **endothermic**. Describe how you can classify a reaction as exothermic or endothermic. Use an example of a chemical reaction to illustrate one of these terms.

🖉 *The quality of written communication will be assessed in your answer to this question.* [6]

(b) Give a safety factor that industrial chemists would need to consider if a synthetic pathway for the manufacture of a chemical involved a highly exothermic reaction. [1]

5. Complete the following paragraph. Use words from this list. [5]

cost	**crystallise**	**desiccator**	**dissolve**
purified	**refrigerator**	**risk**	**temperature**

Chemical synthesis means making a chemical. There are several steps to making a chemical. First, research chemists choose a sequence of reactions that will make the product. Second, a

_____ assessment is carried out to ensure that appropriate safety precautions are

taken. Chemists then work out the quantity of reactants to use and carry out the reaction in suitable

apparatus at the right conditions, for example, concentration and _____. The

product is then separated from the reaction mixture, using a technique such as filtration. The product

must then be _____ to make sure that it is not contaminated by unreacted

reactants or unwanted products. One way to do this is to evaporate any unwanted water by heating the

solution and then leaving the product to _____. The damp crystals can then be

dried in an oven or _____.

6. Emily is investigating antacid tablets. Antacid tablets are taken by people who have acid indigestion. The ingredients listed on the packet include calcium carbonate and magnesium carbonate.

(a) Emily adds a tablet to three different liquids and tests the pH of the solution using universal indicator before and after adding the tablet. She also records her observations. Her results are shown in the table.

Liquid	Colour of Universal Indicator Before Adding Tablet	Colour of Universal Indicator After Adding Tablet	Observations
Water	Green	Green	No evidence of a reaction.
Sodium hydroxide	Dark purple	Dark purple	No evidence of a reaction.
Hydrochloric acid	Red	Green	Fizzing. Tablet appears to dissolve.

(i) Suggest a pH value for the sodium hydroxide solution. [1]

....

(ii) How do Emily's observations prove that these tablets would be effective as a treatment for acid indigestion? [2]

....

....

(b) Melissa also investigated antacid tablets. She compared three different tablets to see which was the best. She added the antacid tablets to separate beakers of dilute hydrochloric acid and measured the pH of the solution that was left after each reaction had finished.

(i) Suggest **two** things that Melissa must do in order to make this a fair test. [2]

1. ....

2. ....

(ii) Here are Melissa's results:

Antacid Brand	pH Before Adding Tablet	pH After Adding Tablet
Acideze	1	4
Peptocool	1	6
Gastrocalm	1	5

Which antacid is the best at neutralising stomach acid? Explain your answer. [2]

....

....

(c) One of the active ingredients in these antacid treatments is calcium carbonate. Complete the word equation for the reaction of calcium carbonate with hydrochloric acid. [1]

Calcium carbonate + Hydrochloric acid ⟶ .... + ... + ...

(d) Another common ingredient in antacid treatments is magnesium carbonate. Josh knows that magnesium metal will react with hydrochloric acid to produce a neutral salt. Why is eating a tablet with magnesium metal in it dangerous, whereas eating a tablet containing magnesium carbonate is much safer? Use **two** word equations in your answer. [5]

....

....

....

....

....

....

7. Use the periodic table on page 97 for this question.

When calcium carbonate is heated, it thermally decomposes to form calcium oxide and carbon dioxide, as shown in the following equation:

Calcium carbonate ⟶ Calcium oxide + Carbon dioxide

$$CaCO_3 \longrightarrow CaO + CO_2$$

The theoretical yield (mass) of calcium oxide that could be produced can be calculated using the following formula, where RFM = relative formula mass:

$$\text{Theoretical yield of calcium oxide} = \frac{\text{Mass of calcium carbonate}}{\text{RFM of calcium carbonate}} \times \text{RFM of calcium oxide}$$

(a) Use the formula to work out the theoretical yield (mass) of calcium oxide that could be formed when 200g of calcium carbonate ($CaCO_3$) is heated. [2]

....

....

....

.... g

(b) Magnesium nitrate, $Mg(NO_3)_2$, was made by reacting an acid with magnesium oxide. The theoretical yield was 12g but the actual yield was 8g.

(i) State the acid needed to make the product. [1]

....

(ii) Calculate the percentage yield. [2]

....

....

....

.... %

8. The diagram shows the apparatus used to perform a titration.

(a) Label the diagram. [3]

(i) ....

(ii) ....

(iii) ....

C6 | Chemical Synthesis

(b) Complete the following method for a titration between an aqueous alkali and an aqueous acid using the words below. [5]

burette   **conical flask**   **drop**   **distilled**   **neutralised**   **squirt**

1. Use a volumetric pipette to accurately measure 25cm³ of alkali and put it into a

   ....

2. Add two drops of indicator and note the colour it goes in the alkali.

3. Carefully fill a .... with your acid solution and make sure that it is at zero.

4. Slowly add the acid to the alkali while you carefully swirl the flask to mix the reactants together.

5. As you notice the colour of the indicator start to change, add the acid one

   .... at a time until the indicator changes colour permanently. The alkali

   has now been .... Record the volume of acid used.

6. If you are using a solid acid, you would first need to dissolve it into a measured volume of

   .... water.

(c) In a titration between sodium hydroxide (NaOH) and hydrochloric acid (HCl), the concentration of the alkali can be calculated using the following formula:

$$\text{Concentration of NaOH (mol/dm}^3) = \frac{\text{Volume of HCl (cm}^3) \times \text{Concentration of HCl (mol/dm}^3)}{\text{Volume of NaOH (cm}^3)}$$

Use this formula to calculate the concentration of NaOH if 25cm³ of NaOH required 20cm³ of HCl to neutralise it. The HCl had a concentration of 0.15mol/dm³. [2]

....

.... mol/dm³

9. **(a)** Explain what is meant by the term **rate of reaction**. [1]

....

....

(b) Why is it important for chemists to be able to control the rate of a reaction? [2]

....

....

....

(c) Which of these is **not** a method of measuring the rate of a reaction? Put a tick (✓) in the box next to the **incorrect** method. [1]

Collecting a gas ◯   Smelling the reaction mixture ◯

Weighing the reaction mixture ◯   Observing the formation of a precipitate ◯

10. (a) State **four** ways to speed up a chemical reaction. [4]

1. ....

2. ....

3. ....

4. ....

(b) Put a tick (✓) in the correct box to show whether each statement about catalysts is **true** or **false**. [4]

	true	false
They are used up in the reaction.	◯	◯
They are always solids.	◯	◯
They are chemically unchanged at the end of the reaction.	◯	◯
They reduce the amount of energy needed by the reactants.	◯	◯

(c) Complete the following paragraph. Use words from this list. [3]

activation   **atomic**   **collision**   **energy**   **maximum**

We can explain the way that some factors affect the speed of a reaction using

.... theory. This theory states that for particles to react, they must collide

with enough .... This amount is called the .... energy.

(d) Explain how increasing the concentration of an aqueous reactant and grinding up lumps of a solid reactant increase the reaction rate. Use ideas about particles and collisions in your answer.

🖉 *The quality of written communication will be assessed in your answer to this question.* [6]

....

....

....

....

....

....

....

C6 | Chemical Synthesis

11. Nick carried out an investigation into the reaction between magnesium and excess hydrochloric acid. He measured the total volume of gas produced by the reaction every ten seconds. His data are in the table below.

Time (s)	Volume of Gas (cm³)
0	0
10	24
20	36
30	43
40	46
50	47
60	47
70	47
80	47
90	47
100	47

(a) Plot a graph to show his results. [2]

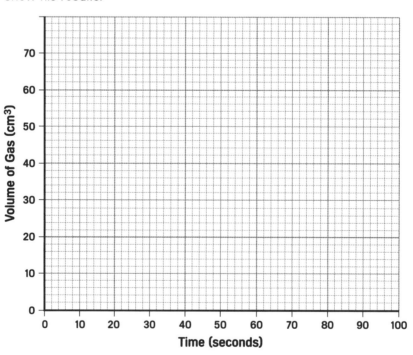

(b) After how many seconds did the reaction stop? [1]

.... seconds

(c) What was the total volume of gas produced? [1]

.... cm^3

(d) On the graph, sketch another line to show the results you would expect to see if Nick repeated his experiment with the same volume and concentration of acid and the same amount of magnesium, but this time at a higher temperature. Label your line **Hot**. [2]

(e) On the graph, sketch another line to show the results you would expect if Nick repeated his experiment at the same temperature but with half as much magnesium. Label your line **Half**. [1]

[Total: .... / 102]

Higher Tier

12. Ryan wants to make some potassium sulfate, which is a salt used in some fertilisers.

Ryan knows that he can make a salt by reacting a metal with an acid.

Ryan
The simplest way to make potassium sulfate is to react potassium with sulfuric acid.

Jack
Reacting potassium with sulfuric acid would be dangerous because there is a lot of water in sulfuric acid.

(a) Use your knowledge of the reaction with water of elements in Group 1 of the periodic table to predict what Ryan would **see** if he added potassium to a dilute solution of sulfuric acid. [2]

....

....

(b) Ryan follows Jack's advice and uses a different method to make the potassium sulfate, starting with potassium hydroxide.

(i) Balance the symbol equation for the reaction. [1]

.... KOH + ... H$_2$SO$_4$ ⟶ .... K$_2$SO$_4$ + ... H$_2$O

(ii) Draw straight lines to show the positive and negative ions present in potassium hydroxide and sulfuric acid. [4]

Positive ions	Reactants	Negative ions

Positive ions:
- H^+
- P^+
- H^{2+}
- K^+
- K^{2+}

Reactants:
- Potassium hydroxide
- Sulfuric acid

Negative ions:
- Cl^-
- OH^-
- O^{2-}
- S^{2-}
- SO_4^{2-}

(iii) Ryan asks his friends to help him understand the reaction. Below are some of his friends' comments. Put a tick (✓) in the correct box to show whether each statement is **true** or **false**. [4]

	true	false
The reaction is a neutralisation reaction.	☐	☐
You can tell when the reaction has finished because it will stop fizzing.	☐	☐
The ionic equation for this reaction is $H^+ + OH^- \longrightarrow H_2O$.	☐	☐
All acids contain OH^- ions.	☐	☐

13. Energy changes in reactions can be represented by energy-level diagrams. Draw energy-level diagrams to show an endothermic reaction and an exothermic reaction. Label your diagrams with the words **reactants** and **products**. [3]

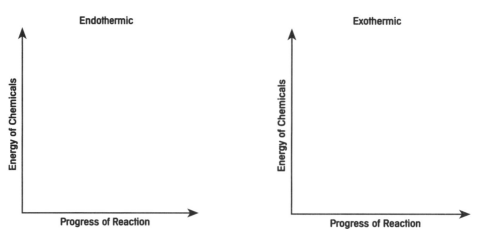

14. Emily is planning to do the thermite reaction, which involves displacing iron from iron oxide (Fe_2O_3) using aluminium powder. The other product of the reaction is aluminium oxide (Al_2O_3).

(a) Represent this reaction as a balanced symbol equation. [2]

_____

(b) Calculate the relative formula masses (RFMs) of Fe_2O_3 and Al_2O_3.

(i) Fe_2O_3: _____ [1]

(ii) Al_2O_3: _____ [1]

(c) If Emily starts with 16g of Fe_2O_3, what mass of aluminium should she weigh out for the reaction? [2]

_____

_____

_____ g

(d) What is the theoretical yield of iron in Emily's reaction? [2]

_____

_____

_____ g

15. Simone is investigating the thermal decomposition of copper carbonate. When she heats the solid in a boiling tube, it breaks down forming copper oxide and releasing carbon dioxide.

$$CuCO_3(s) \longrightarrow CuO(s) + CO_2(g)$$

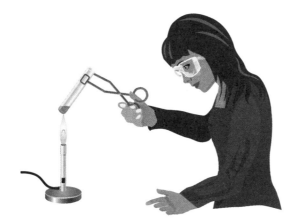

(a) Simone measures the mass of the boiling tube and the powder before the experiment and after she has heated it for ten minutes. She finds that the mass has decreased. Suggest why the mass has decreased. [1]

_____

(b) Simone wants to work out the theoretical yield of carbon dioxide, so she calculates the relative formula mass of each compound using relative atomic masses from the periodic table.

Element	Relative Atomic Mass
Copper	63.5
Carbon	12
Oxygen	16

Simone writes her calculated values for the relative formula masses underneath the formulae in the symbol equation. Write the missing value in the space provided. [1]

$CuCO_3$ $\longrightarrow$ CuO + CO_2

.... 79.5 44

(c) Simone also investigates nickel carbonate, $NiCO_3$, which reacts in a similar way. The relative formula mass of each compound has been written underneath each formula in the balanced symbol equation below.

$NiCO_3$ $\longrightarrow$ NiO + CO_2

119 75 44

Simone weighs out 1.19g of nickel carbonate into a boiling tube. What is the theoretical yield of carbon dioxide? [1]

....

.... g

(d) Simone then investigates manganese carbonate. She calculates that by heating 1.5g of manganese carbonate she should produce 0.57g of carbon dioxide. After the experiment, she calculates that 0.40g of carbon dioxide was released. Calculate the percentage yield of her experiment. [2]

....

....

.... %

[Total: .... / 27]

1.   **(a)** Which of the following shows the functional group of a carboxylic acid? Put a (ring) around the correct answer.   [1]

$$C=C \qquad -OH \qquad -COOH \qquad -Cl$$

(b) Vinegar is a dilute solution of ethanoic acid. What is its formula?   [1]

....

(c) Which of the following statements about carboxylic acids are true? Put ticks (✓) in the boxes next to the **two** correct answers.   [2]

Carboxylic acids smell fruity.   ☐

Carboxylic acids have a pH of between 1 and 2.   ☐

Carboxylic acids are used as fruit flavourings in some foods.   ☐

A molecule of methanoic acid is made up of three different types of atom.   ☐

Carboxylic acids react with metals to produce a salt and hydrogen gas.   ☐

(d) Carboxylic acids behave in the same way as strong acids such as hydrochloric acid. They are neutralised by bases to produce salts. Complete the following word equation.   [1]

Ethanoic acid + Sodium carbonate ⟶ Sodium ethanoate + ... + ...

(e) Esters are sweet-smelling chemicals that are responsible for the smells and flavours of fruits. They are formed when carboxylic acids react with alcohols.

   (i) Suggest **two** uses of esters.   [2]

   1. ....

   2. ....

   (ii) Complete the following word equation.   [2]

   Ethanoic acid + ... ⟶ Ethyl ethanoate + ...

2. **(a)** Which of the following compounds are hydrocarbons? Put ticks (✓) in the boxes next
to the **two** correct answers. [2]

CH_3Cl ⬭

CH_3OH ⬭

C_2H_4 ⬭

CH_2O ⬭

C_4H_{10} ⬭

CH_3CH_2COOH ⬭

(b) Complete the following sentences. Use words from this list. [3]

saturated   **unsaturated**   **single**   **double**   **more**   **less**

Alkanes are also known as .... hydrocarbons because all the

carbon–carbon bonds are .... This makes them ....

reactive than .... hydrocarbons, which contain a ....

reactive .... bond.

(c) Write down the molecular formulae of the following compounds.

Key: ◯ Hydrogen   ⬤ Carbon   ◗ Oxygen

(i) Ethanol .... [1]

(ii) .... [1]

(iii) .... [1]

(iv) .... [1]

(d) A hydrocarbon burning in a good supply of air will always produce carbon dioxide and water.
Using a named hydrocarbon, write a word equation to represent this reaction. [2]

.... + ... ⟶ .... + ...

3. (a) Organic molecules have many applications. Which of the following use methanol as a feedstock? Put ticks (✓) in the boxes next to the **three** correct answers. [3]

Food flavourings ⬜

Fuel ⬜

Alcoholic drinks ⬜

Adhesives ⬜

Vinegar ⬜

(b) Which of the following statements are true? Put ticks (✓) in the boxes next to the **four** correct answers. [4]

An alcohol will have a lower boiling point than a similar alkane. ⬜

Alcohols are less dense than water. ⬜

It is the −OH group in a molecule of an alcohol that is attracted to a molecule of water. ⬜

Carboxylic acids are responsible for the taste of rancid butter. ⬜

Esters are responsible for the smell of a sweaty training shoe. ⬜

Fats and oils are used by living organisms as an energy store. ⬜

(c) Many adverts claim that spreads made from vegetable oils are better for you than butter because they are high in polyunsaturated fats.

(i) What are polyunsaturated fats? [2]

(ii) Suggest why adverts claim that polyunsaturated fats are better for you than saturated fats. [2]

4. Chemicals made on a large scale are often referred to as 'bulk' chemicals, whereas those made on a small scale are referred to as 'fine' chemicals.

(a) Which are fine chemicals? Put ticks (✓) in the boxes next to the **two** correct answers. [2]

Ammonia ◯   Sodium hydroxide ◯

Food additives ◯   Fragrances ◯

(b) Statements **A** to **E** show the various stages in the production of chemicals. They are not in the correct order. Put the statements in the correct order by writing the letters in the empty boxes. One has been done for you. [3]

A Synthesis

B Monitoring purity

C Preparation of feedstocks

D Handling of by-products and waste

E Separation of products

Start					**B**

(c) Why is it important for the chemical industry to follow strict Government health and safety guidance? [2]

....

....

(d) All hazardous chemicals need to be labelled with standard hazard symbols. A tanker transporting a chemical is labelled with the following symbols:

Use the hazard symbols to help decide what safety precautions should be taken during the transportation of the chemical.

✎ *The quality of written communication will be assessed in your answer to this question.* [6]

....

....

....

....

....

....

5. Several types of suncream with an advertised sun protection factor (SPF) of 16 were tested. The results are shown in the table below. To be approved for use they need to have the advertised sun protection factor and cause no adverse effects.

Feature	Suncream A	Suncream B	Suncream C	Suncream D	Suncream E
Flow	Hard to apply (thin liquid)	Easy to apply	Easy to apply	Hard to apply (thick liquid)	Easy to apply
SPF	16	10	8	16	16
Reaction with skin	No reaction	No reaction	No reaction	May irritate sensitive skin	No reaction
Water resistance	Remains effective for 5 minutes	Remains effective for 40 minutes	Remains effective for 40 minutes	Remains effective for 60 minutes	Remains effective for 35 minutes

(a) Would suncream D and suncream E be approved? Explain your answer. [4]

(b) Suggest how the public would respond if suncream C was approved and put on the market. Explain your answer. [3]

6. Ethanoic acid is an important bulk chemical, with over 8 million tonnes being produced every year.

Over the years the chemical industry has modified the production method to make it more sustainable. The table below summarises two methods of production.

	Pre-1970s Method	The Monsanto Process
Main reaction	Oxidation of hydrocarbons	Methanol + Carbon monoxide ➞ Ethanoic acid
Feedstock	Crude oil	Carbon monoxide and hydrogen or biomass
Operating conditions	Temperature 180–200°C Pressure 40–50 atmospheres	Temperature 150–180°C Pressure 30–60 atmospheres A catalyst made from rhodium metal and iodide ions
Atom economy	35%	100%

(a) Which method uses the more sustainable feedstock? Explain your answer. [4]

....

....

....

....

....

....

(b) What does the atom economy tell us about the waste involved in each of these reactions and the implications of it? [4]

....

....

....

....

....

....

....

(c) Which statements about catalysts are true? Put ticks (✓) in the boxes next to the **two** correct answers. [2]

The catalyst gets used up during the reaction. ⬭

The catalyst makes the reaction exothermic. ⬭

The catalyst lowers the activation energy of the reaction. ⬭

The catalyst heats up the reaction. ⬭

The catalyst speeds up the reaction without being chemically changed at the end of it. ⬭

(d) In 1986, BP bought the rights to the Monsanto process and spent a lot of time and money carrying out research into different catalysts. BP later started to use a modified version of the Monsanto process called the Cativa process. The main difference was that iridium metal replaced the rhodium metal in the catalyst.

Suggest why BP decided to spend time and money researching catalysts. [2]

(e) Today, some countries still use the pre-1970s method to produce ethanoic acid. Do you think that this should be allowed? You must support your answer with clear arguments and explanations.

🖉 *The quality of written communication will be assessed in your answer to this question.* [6]

7. **(a)** Which of the acids below are examples of weak acids? Put ticks (✓) in the boxes next to the **three** correct answers. [3]

Hydrobromic acid ◯

Citric acid ◯

Sulfuric acid ◯

Methanoic acid ◯

Butanoic acid ◯

Nitric acid ◯

(b) Which of the following statements is true? Put a tick (✓) in the box next to the correct answer. [1]

A weak acid is less reactive than hydrochloric acid. ◯

All acids have a pH greater than 7. ◯

A dilute acid is the same as a weak acid. ◯

Ethanoic acid has a pH of 1. ◯

(c) Vinegar is a dilute solution of a weak acid called ethanoic acid. Dilute hydrochloric acid is a strong acid.

Is the following statement true or false? Use ideas about ions to help explain your answer.

'Dilute solutions of weak acids have higher pH values than dilute solutions of strong acids.' [4]

8. **(a)** Complete the following paragraph. Use words from this list. [4]

activation   **endothermic**   **energy**   **exothermic**

less   **more**   **sound**

Exothermic reactions release _____, usually in the form of heat. It is often easy

to identify exothermic reactions in the laboratory because you can detect a rise in temperature.

Examples of exothermic reactions include when magnesium reacts with acid and when fuels burn.

Reactions that take in energy are called _____ reactions and often feel cold to

the touch. All reactions need to absorb some energy to start them off and this is called the

_____ energy. It is used to start breaking the bonds in the reactants. Once this

has been done, new bonds can be formed in the products, which is an exothermic process, so it

releases energy. If the total amount of energy needed to break the bonds in the reactants is

_____ than the total amount of energy released when new bonds are made, the

reaction is exothermic.

(b) Look at the table of data below.

	Temperature at Start (°C)	Temperature at End (°C)
Reaction A	22	16
Reaction B	24	31

Which reaction is endothermic? _____ [1]

9. **(a)** Write the symbol used to show that a reaction is reversible. [1]

_____

(b) What happens to a reversible reaction if it is kept in a closed system and left for a long period of
time? Put a tick (✓) in the box next to the correct answer. [1]

It stops. ◯   It goes back to the start. ◯

It reaches a dynamic equilibrium. ◯   It explodes. ◯

(c) What bulk chemical is made in the Haber process? [1]

_____

(d) (i) Write a word equation showing the formation of ammonia in the Haber process. [2]

....

(ii) Write a symbol equation showing the formation of ammonia (NH_3) in the Haber process. You do not need to balance the equation. [2]

....

(e) Label the flow diagram for the Haber process. Use words from this list. [3]

burnt   **limestone**   **natural gas**   **nitrogen**   **oxygen**   **recycled**

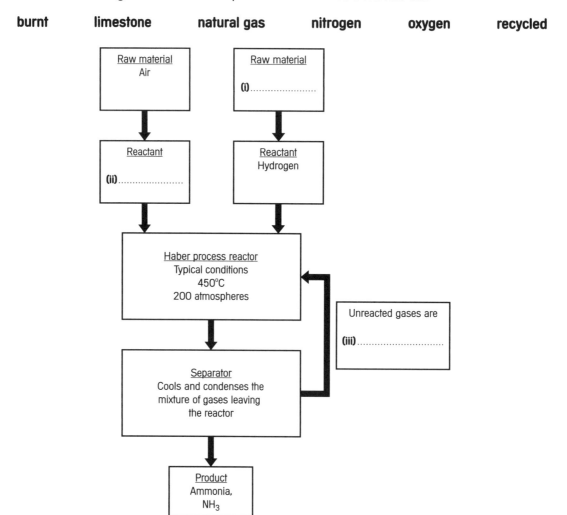

(f) Look at the graph.

(i) What effect does increasing the pressure have on the yield of ammonia? [1]

....

(ii) What effect does increasing the temperature have on the yield of ammonia? [1]

....

10. (a) Complete the following paragraph. Use words from this list. [4]

| decreasing | endothermic | exothermic | greater |
| increasing | lower | recycling | wasting |

In the Haber process, the higher the pressure, the _____ the yield. This explains

why the plant operates at a high pressure. The yield is also improved by _____

the unreacted nitrogen and hydrogen that leave the reactor. Increasing the temperature has the effect

of _____ the yield, because the forwards reaction is _____ ,

so increasing the temperature favours the reverse reaction.

(b) The Haber process is an artificial way of 'fixing' atmospheric nitrogen. Describe how nitrogen
can be fixed by natural processes. [3]

....

....

....

....

(c) Why is it important for nitrogen to be fixed? [1]

....

11. Chemists are interested in finding a new catalyst for the Haber process. They are focusing their
research on enzymes. Suggest why. Use your understanding of how catalysts work in your answer.

🖉 *The quality of written communication will be assessed in your answer to this question.* [6]

....

....

....

....

....

....

....

....

12. **(a)** Describe the difference between **qualitative** and **quantitative** methods of analysis. Give two examples of qualitative analysis and one example of quantitative analysis.

✎ The quality of written communication will be assessed in your answer to this question. [6]

(b) During analysis, why is it important to test a sample that represents the bulk of the material? [1]

(c) During analysis, it is very important that standard procedures are followed for the collection, storage and preparation of samples. What is meant by the term **standard procedures**? [1]

13. **(a)** What is meant by the term **non-aqueous** when applied to a solvent in chromatography? [1]

(b) Describe the stages in paper chromatography. Use the words below in your answer.

mobile phase **stationary phase**

✎ The quality of written communication will be assessed in your answer to this question. [6]

(c) Give **two** advantages of thin layer chromatography over paper chromatography. [2]

1. ....

2. ....

(d) What is a **locating agent** in chromatography and what is it used for? [1]

....

....

(e) (i) Look at the thin layer chromatogram. Calculate the R_f value of the four compounds on the chromatogram. [4]

Solvent front

Baseline

Mystery compound   Cocaine   Heroin   Laundry powder

Mystery compound: ....

Cocaine: ....

Heroin: ....

Laundry powder: ....

(ii) Use the chromatogram to suggest the identity of the mystery compound. [1]

....

(f) Other than by comparing it to other chemicals on the chromatogram, how can the R_f value of a mystery compound be used to verify its identity? [1]

....

....

14. (a) Complete the following paragraph. Use words from this list. [5]

cooled   **heated**   **mobile**   **quickly**   **retention**   **slowly**   **stationary**

In gas chromatography, the .... phase is an unreactive carrier gas and the

.... phase is a very thin layer of liquid on an unreactive solid support. The

sample is .... to evaporate it and then passed into the column in the carrier

gas. Substances that have a greater affinity for the mobile phase pass through the column

.... and have a short .... time. Substances that have

a greater affinity for the stationary phase take much longer to pass through the column, so are

detected at the end of the column some time later.

(b) Look at the gas chromatogram of an athlete's urine sample.

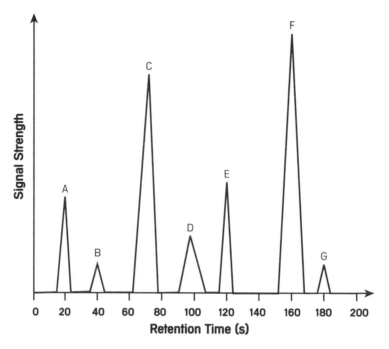

(i) How many compounds were detected by this analysis? [1]

....

(ii) What is the retention time of compound C? [1]

.... seconds

(iii) Which compound is present in the greatest amount? [1]

....

(iv) Which compound has the shortest retention time? [1]

....

(v) Which compound has the longest retention time? [1]

....

(vi) A banned drug has a retention time of 140 seconds. Suggest, with a reason, whether this athlete is guilty of taking performance-enhancing drugs. [1]

....

....

....

15. **(a)** Draw straight lines to show the use in a titration of each piece of laboratory apparatus. [3]

Apparatus	Use
Pipette	Holds the burette securely and vertically
Burette	Allows the colour change of the indicator to be seen easily
White tile	Used to measure a specific volume of liquid which goes in the conical flask
Clamp and stand	Used to accurately measure the volume of the second reactant added

(b) Give **one** unit that can be used to measure the concentration of a solution. [1]

(c) Why is it considered good practice to carry out a titration at least three times? [1]

(d) Other than an indicator, what could be used to detect the end point of a titration? [1]

16. **(a)** Here are some steps used to quantitatively analyse a solid acid by titration with a known concentration of alkali. They are not in the correct order. Put the steps in the correct order by writing the letters in the empty boxes. Three have been done for you. [4]

A Dissolve the solid acid in distilled water and make up to $250cm^3$.

B Add the acid from the burette to the alkali until the colour of the indicator begins to change.

C Weigh out 10g of solid acid using an accurate balance.

D Fill a burette with acid solution and measure $25cm^3$ of the alkali into a conical flask using a pipette.

E Repeat the experiment to ensure your results are reliable.

F Add two drops of indicator to the conical flask.

G Add the acid drop by drop until you see the colour of the indicator change permanently.

H Note the volume of acid used.

Start	C		D					E

(b) Alex carried out a titration between potassium hydroxide and 0.1mol/dm³ hydrochloric acid. Each time, he used 25cm³ of potassium hydroxide. Here are his results:

	Start Volume (cm³)	End Volume (cm³)	Titre (cm³)
Rough	0.0	26.1	
Titration 1	26.1	51.3	
Titration 2	1.0	26.6	
Titration 3	3.5	29.4	

(i) Complete the table by calculating the titre values. [4]

(ii) Are Alex's results sufficient for him to analyse his data? Explain your answer. [2]

(c) Gill repeated the titration. Here are her results:

	Start Volume (cm³)	End Volume (cm³)	Titre (cm³)
Rough	0.0	25.9	
Titration 1	1.5	26.6	
Titration 2	0.3	25.6	
Titration 3	2.1	27.4	

(i) Complete the table by calculating the titre values. [4]

(ii) Calculate the average titre value from Gill's results. Show your working. [3]

.... cm³

(iii) For this titration, the concentration of the potassium hydroxide (KOH) can be calculated using the following formula:

$$\text{Concentration of KOH (mol/dm}^3) = \frac{\text{Average volume of HCl (cm}^3) \times 0.1}{25}$$

Calculate the concentration of KOH using Gill's data. [2]

.... mol/dm³

(d) When titrating sodium hydroxide (NaOH) with sulfuric acid (H_2SO_4), you can use the following formula to find the concentration of the sulfuric acid:

$$\text{Concentration of } H_2SO_4 \text{ (mol/dm}^3) = \frac{\text{Volume of NaOH (cm}^3) \times \text{Concentration of NaOH (mol/dm}^3)}{2 \times \text{Volume of } H_2SO_4 \text{ (cm}^3)}$$

If 25cm³ of NaOH, which has a concentration of 1.5mol/dm³, requires 30cm³ of H_2SO_4 to neutralise it, what is the concentration of the acid? [2]

....

....

.... mol/dm³

17. Five different students analysed the same sample of vinegar to find the concentration of ethanoic acid. They all followed the same standard procedures. Here are their results:

   11.4g/dm³   **11.8g/dm³**   **10.9g/dm³**   **11.4g/dm³**   **11.1g/dm³**

(a) (i) What is meant by an **outlier**? [1]

....

....

(ii) Are any of these results outliers? [1]

....

(b) What is the average (mean) result? Show your working. [2]

....

.... g/dm³

(c) Complete this statement to show the range.

The range is from .... g/dm³ to .... g/dm³. [1]

(d) What is the overall uncertainty? [1]

....

(e) Calculate the percentage error. [2]

....

....

.... %

[Total: .... / 178]

18. The laboratory preparation of an ester takes place in four distinct stages.

A Purification   **B** Reflux

C Distillation   **D** Drying

(a) The stages are not in the correct order. Put the stages in the correct order by writing the letters in the empty boxes. [2]

Start	**B**			

(b) Which two stages use the apparatus shown below? [2]

(i) ....   **(ii)** ....

(c) During the reflux stage a few drops of concentrated sulfuric acid are added to the carboxylic acid and alcohol mixture.

(i) Explain what is meant by the term **heat under reflux**. [2]

....

....

(ii) Suggest a reason for adding a few drops of concentrated sulfuric acid to the mixture. [2]

....

....

(d) Describe what happens during the purification stage. [2]

....

....

....

(e) Anhydrous calcium chloride is used during the drying stage. Explain why it is used and how it is removed at the end of the reaction. [2]

....

....

....

....

19. The chemical industry is always looking for new ways to make chemical reactions greener and more efficient. Both the percentage yield and the atom economy are calculated for reactions during the research and development stage. They are calculated using the following formulae:

$$\text{Percentage yield} = \frac{\text{Actual yield}}{\text{Theoretical yield}} \times 100$$

$$\text{Atom economy} = \frac{\text{Mass of atoms in the product}}{\text{Mass of atoms in the reactants}} \times 100$$

(a) Describe the difference between the terms **percentage yield** and **atom economy**. [4]

....

....

....

....

(b) Sodium ethanoate is used in the production of some dyed textiles and leather goods. It is a product of the following reaction:

Ethanoic acid + Sodium carbonate $\longrightarrow$ Sodium ethanoate + Carbon dioxide + Water

$2CH_3COOH + Na_2CO_3 \longrightarrow 2CH_3COONa + CO_2 + H_2O$

When a technician carried out this reaction in the laboratory, he started with 30g of ethanoic acid and produced 31g of sodium ethanoate.

(i) Calculate the percentage yield. [2]

....

....

....

....

....

.... %

(ii) Explain why it is not possible to obtain a yield of 100%. [3]

....

....

....

....

....

(iii) Calculate the atom economy for the reaction. [2]

....

....

....

.... %

(iv) What is the percentage of waste products in this reaction? [1]

....

20. **(a)** Which of the following shows the functional group of an alcohol? Put a tick (✓) in the box next to the correct answer. [1]

C=C ☐

−OH ☐

−COOH ☐

−Cl ☐

(b) Alcohols can behave like alkanes because they contain a hydrocarbon chain. Write a balanced symbol equation, including state symbols, to show the complete combustion of liquid ethanol (C_2H_5OH) to form water vapour and carbon dioxide. [3]

....

....

(c) The −OH functional group allows alcohols to 'behave like water'. Describe what would happen if sodium was added to ethanol. [2]

(d) Complete the word equation for the reaction in part **(c)**. [1]

Sodium + Ethanol ⟶ .... + Hydrogen

(e) (i) How would you expect the reaction with sodium to differ if water was used instead of ethanol? [2]

(ii) Write a balanced symbol equation for the reaction. Include the state symbols. [4]

21. Draw an energy-level diagram for an exothermic reaction. Label the activation energy for the reaction and the overall energy change. [3]

22. The table below shows some bond energies.

Bond	Bond Energy (kJ/mol)
H–H	436
I–I	151
H–I	298
H–O	463
O=O	496

(a) (i) Use the bond energies given in the table to calculate the energy change for the following reaction.

$H_2 + I_2 \longrightarrow 2HI$ [2]

....

....

....

.... kJ/mol

(ii) Is the reaction between hydrogen and iodine exothermic or endothermic? [1]

....

(b) (i) Use the bond energies in the table to calculate the energy change for the following reaction. [2]

$2H_2 + O_2 \longrightarrow 2H_2O$

....

....

....

.... kJ/mol

(ii) Is the reaction between hydrogen and oxygen exothermic or endothermic? [1]

....

23. **(a)** When a reversible reaction has reached a dynamic equilibrium, what can be said about the rate of the forwards and reverse reactions? [1]

....

(b) In the Haber process, chemists try to maximise the yield of ammonia and the rate of the reaction. The conditions chosen are often described as a **compromise**. Explain why this is.

🖉 *The quality of written communication will be assessed in your answer to this question.* [6]

....

....

....

....

....

....

....

....

....

....

24. **(a)** A standard solution of sodium hydroxide was made by dissolving 10g of solid sodium hydroxide in 250cm^3 of distilled water. Work out the concentration in g/dm^3. [2]

....

....

.... g/dm^3

(b) Pam measured out 25.0cm^3 of sodium carbonate solution, which had a concentration of 60g/dm^3, and poured it into a clean beaker. What mass of sodium carbonate was present in the beaker? [2]

....

....

.... g

25. Imran wanted to work out the concentration of a solution of potassium hydroxide using a $1.0mol/dm^3$ solution of nitric acid. The balanced symbol equation is shown below.

$$KOH + HNO_3 \longrightarrow KNO_3 + H_2O$$

Imran placed $20cm^3$ of the potassium hydroxide in a conical flask with a suitable indicator and then added the nitric acid from a burette. His results are in the table below.

	Start Volume (cm^3)	End Volume (cm^3)	Titre (cm^3)
Rough	0.0	16.0	
Titration 1	0.6	15.2	
Titration 2	1.9	16.8	
Titration 3	4.5	19.5	

(a) Complete the table by calculating the titre values. [4]

(b) Select the appropriate titre values and then calculate an average. Give your answer to two decimal places. Clearly show in your working which titre values you use. [2]

....

....

.... cm^3

(c) Work out the concentration of the potassium hydroxide, using your answer to part **(b)**, the balanced equation and the information given above. [2]

....

....

.... mol/dm^3

[Total: .... / 65]

Periodic Table

Key

relative atomic mass
atomic symbol
name
atomic (proton) number

1	2		3	4	5	6	7	0
								4 **He** helium 2
7 **Li** lithium 3	9 **Be** beryllium 4		11 **B** boron 5	12 **C** carbon 6	14 **N** nitrogen 7	16 **O** oxygen 8	19 **F** fluorine 9	20 **Ne** neon 10
23 **Na** sodium 11	24 **Mg** magnesium 12		27 **Al** aluminium 13	28 **Si** silicon 14	31 **P** phosphorus 15	32 **S** sulfur 16	35.5 **Cl** chlorine 17	40 **Ar** argon 18

1 **H** hydrogen 1

1	2											3	4	5	6	7	0
39 **K** potassium 19	40 **Ca** calcium 20	45 **Sc** scandium 21	48 **Ti** titanium 22	51 **V** vanadium 23	52 **Cr** chromium 24	55 **Mn** manganese 25	56 **Fe** iron 26	59 **Co** cobalt 27	59 **Ni** nickel 28	63.5 **Cu** copper 29	65 **Zn** zinc 30	70 **Ga** gallium 31	73 **Ge** germanium 32	75 **As** arsenic 33	79 **Se** selenium 34	80 **Br** bromine 35	84 **Kr** krypton 36
85 **Rb** rubidium 37	88 **Sr** strontium 38	89 **Y** yttrium 39	91 **Zr** zirconium 40	93 **Nb** niobium 41	96 **Mo** molybdenum 42	[98] **Tc** technetium 43	101 **Ru** ruthenium 44	103 **Rh** rhodium 45	106 **Pd** palladium 46	108 **Ag** silver 47	112 **Cd** cadmium 48	115 **In** indium 49	119 **Sn** tin 50	122 **Sb** antimony 51	128 **Te** tellurium 52	127 **I** iodine 53	131 **Xe** xenon 54
133 **Cs** caesium 55	137 **Ba** barium 56	139 **La*** lanthanum 57	178 **Hf** hafnium 72	181 **Ta** tantalum 73	184 **W** tungsten 74	186 **Re** rhenium 75	190 **Os** osmium 76	192 **Ir** iridium 77	195 **Pt** platinum 78	197 **Au** gold 79	201 **Hg** mercury 80	204 **Tl** thallium 81	207 **Pb** lead 82	209 **Bi** bismuth 83	[209] **Po** polonium 84	[210] **At** astatine 85	[222] **Rn** radon 86
[223] **Fr** francium 87	[226] **Ra** radium 88	[227] **Ac*** actinium 89	[261] **Rf** rutherfordium 104	[262] **Db** dubnium 105	[266] **Sg** seaborgium 106	[264] **Bh** bohrium 107	[277] **Hs** hassium 108	[268] **Mt** meitnerium 109	[271] **Ds** darmstadtium 110	[272] **Rg** roentgenium 111							

Elements with atomic numbers 112–116 have been reported but not fully authenticated.

*The lanthanoids (atomic numbers 58–71) and the actinoids (atomic numbers 90–103) have been omitted.

The relative atomic masses of copper and chlorine have not been rounded to the nearest whole number.

Data Sheet

Qualitative Analysis

Tests for Positively Charged Ions

Ion	Test	Observation
Calcium Ca^{2+}	Add dilute sodium hydroxide	A white precipitate forms; the precipitate does not dissolve in excess sodium hydroxide
Copper Cu^{2+}	Add dilute sodium hydroxide	A light blue precipitate forms; the precipitate does not dissolve in excess sodium hydroxide
Iron(II) Fe^{2+}	Add dilute sodium hydroxide	A green precipitate forms; the precipitate does not dissolve in excess sodium hydroxide
Iron(III) Fe^{3+}	Add dilute sodium hydroxide	A red-brown precipitate forms; the precipitate does not dissolve in excess sodium hydroxide
Zinc Zn^{2+}	Add dilute sodium hydroxide	A white precipitate forms; the precipitate dissolves in excess sodium hydroxide

Tests for Negatively Charged Ions

Ion	Test	Observation
Carbonate CO_3^{2-}	Add dilute acid	The solution effervesces; carbon dioxide gas is produced (the gas turns limewater from colourless to milky)
Chloride Cl^-	Add dilute nitric acid, then add silver nitrate	A white precipitate forms
Bromide Br^-	Add dilute nitric acid, then add silver nitrate	A cream precipitate forms
Iodide I^-	Add dilute nitric acid, then add silver nitrate	A yellow precipitate forms
Sulfate SO_4^{2-}	Add dilute nitric acid, then add barium chloride or barium nitrate	A white precipitate forms

Notes

Notes